International Developments
in assuring
Quality in Higher Education

International Developments
in assuring
Quality in Higher Education

edited by

Alma Craft

Selected Papers from an
International Conference, Montreal 1993

 The Falmer Press

(A member of the Taylor & Francis Group)
London • Washington, D.C.

UK   The Falmer Press, 4 John Street, London WC1N 2ET
USA   The Falmer Press, Taylor & Francis Inc., 1900 Frost Road, Suite 101, Bristol, PA 19007

First published 1994

A catalogue record for this book is available from the British Library

Library of Congress Cataloging-in-Publication Data are available on request

ISBN 0 7507 0314 8 (cased)
ISBN 0 7507 0315 6 (paper)

Jacket design by Caroline Archer

Typeset in 10/12pt Bembo by
Graphicraft Typesetters Ltd, Hong Kong

Printed in Great Britain by Burgess Science Press, Basingstoke on paper which has a specified pH value on final paper manufacture of not less than 7.5 and is therefore 'acid free'.

Contents

Contents

Foreword

The papers in this publication arose from the 1993 Conference of the International Network of Quality Assurance Agencies in Higher Education (INQAAHE). Held in Montreal, Canada, the Conference was jointly organized by the Conference of Rectors and Principals of Quebec Universities, and the United States Center for Quality Assurance in International Education. It was funded by the Quebec government and the United States Agency for International Development. The INQAAHE secretariat is currently based at the Hong Kong Council for Academic Accreditation, and its next conference will be held in The Netherlands in 1995.

Editor's Introduction

As industrialized and industrializing societies demand increasingly advanced skills, more and more young people and adults are studying for a tertiary level qualification. The importance of providing credible academic and professional awards and the huge cost of this provision whether publicly or privately funded, has prompted national governments and tertiary institutions themselves to establish sophisticated mechanisms to evaluate, assure and improve the quality of the education offered and the awards granted. Added to this, 'globalization' and international migration mean that academic and professional qualifications need to be 'portable' across national borders, and so both institutions and nation states are keen to learn more about each other's procedures for assuring the quality of tertiary education provision.

Quality assurance and quality assessment are consequently high on the agenda in most countries, but the problems faced vary. The West, for example, is concerned to maintain its generally high academic standards while pursuing greater access and opportunity. As it moves towards mass higher education with greater diversity of students and modes, together with tightened resources, quality assurance arrangements seek to balance quantity and quality, institutional autonomy and public accountability. Poorer nations which are still in the process of establishing their higher education systems, and with far more limited resources, are anxious to reach minimal international standards. Countries currently emerging from a history of political centralization are seeking ways of encouraging greater academic freedom and institutional self-evaluation. In each of these different contexts, quality assurance or accreditation agencies which are external to the institutions themselves are increasingly seen as a useful device to guarantee standards, to give a public account of this expensive educational provision, and to enhance quality through the interchange of ideas and practices.

The International Network of Quality Assurance Agencies in Higher Education (INQAAHE) was formed to assist organizations engaged in this. The Network publishes a regular *Newsletter* and has established a database to facilitate links and disseminate information. In 1993 it arranged its first international conference in Montreal, Canada. Some 300 senior academics, and administrators from governments, agencies and institutions in nearly fifty countries attended, with speakers from Africa, North and South America,

Asia, Australia, Western and Eastern Europe, the Middle East and New Zealand.

Conference sessions considered both traditional and newer methods of assuring the quality of tertiary institutions, the standards of academic programmes, the relationship between accountability and academic freedom, and the role of international organizations, as well as the quality issues arising from expansion, resource constraints and the mobility of students, academics and professionals. Nearly a hundred papers were presented at the conference (see Appendix), offering both agency and institutional perspectives. This volume brings together a small selection of these papers, concentrating on national and international developments which take an *external* view of the quality of education provided by public and private tertiary institutions in different parts of the world. The purpose of this collection is to provide an overview of current developments, supplementing the account of international initiatives reviewed in the previous Falmer publication *Quality Assurance in Higher Education* (Craft, 1992) which arose from an earlier conference held in Hong Kong. That quality assurance approaches *within* institutions and institutional responses and reactions to external quality assurance are not addressed here should not be misinterpreted. Internal processes and their interaction with external agencies are indeed matters of critical importance, but were not the main focus of the Montreal conference or of this publication.

The book begins with perspectives from four major regions. Professor Frans van Vught from The Netherlands traces the history of quality assessment from its roots in medieval universities to more recent experiences in North America and Western Europe; and he distinguishes between models which vest control in an external authority and those which are based on a self-governing community of scholars. From this analysis, he proposes a general model which draws on both traditions. Hernan Ayarza provides an overview of university accreditation in Latin America, touching on country-specific legislation, projects and strategies which are trying to maximize the efficiency and effectiveness of rapidly expanding and diversifying higher education systems. In Chapter 3, Grant Harman attempts an overview of quality issues and new directions in the vast Asia-Pacific region which includes some of the world's most dynamic economies as well as some of the poorest nations. And Juma Shabani's chapter describes the battle to maintain standards in African countries, as higher education struggles with massive educational expansion in the context of profound political, social and economic changes and of severe financial constraints.

The second section reviews some recent national developments. Legislation in Chile is introducing institutional accreditation to provide public assurance about academic quality. A Centre for Quality Assurance and Evaluation of Higher Education has been established in Denmark, and the Council for University Accreditation is now the highest authority on university evaluation in Korea. In New Zealand, a national Qualifications Authority coordinates the quality assurance of all secondary and tertiary level qualifications; and in

South Africa, there are proposals to create a national structure bringing together the various accreditation arrangements for vocational higher education. A chapter on Quebec, Canada, describes how new higher education programmes are approved and existing provision audited, both involving a process of academic peer review; and the quality assessment functions of one of the new UK Higher Education Funding Councils is outlined in Chapter 11. A case-study from Romania illustrates some of the developments in Eastern Europe, and a final chapter in this section explains the background to current criticisms of America's long-established system of institutional accreditation through voluntary self-regulation, and how the regional accrediting agencies are responding.

The third section of the book focuses on international activities, and opens with a review of the global links between professional bodies, regional trade agreements and the export of higher education systems and programmes, all of which are underlining the need for consultation and coordination to assure the quality of educational provision and qualifications beyond and between national borders. The franchising of courses by well-established institutions for use in other parts of the world is a relatively recent development, and Chapter 15 presents a case-study involving a UK university and a Malaysian college, suggesting some general principles and a framework for quality assurance in such operations. As technologies develop and the cost of traditional provision escalates, distance education across national and continental borders is expanding, and the implications for institutions, staff and students, and for quality assurance are discussed in Chapter 16.

Chapters 17 and 18 offer perspectives from two international agencies, The World Bank and UNESCO, each actively involved in promoting higher education in industrializing nations. As a financial lending institution, The World Bank stresses the efficient use of scarce national resources. It advocates greater reliance on the private financing of higher education institutions, with the Bank providing technical assistance for the maintenance and improvement of quality in both the public and private sectors. A series of UNESCO regional consultations and international meetings has identified quality assurance as a priority. Recognizing that the developing countries which most need to enhance the quality of their provision have the least resources to do so, some UNESCO initiatives to disseminate expertise and encourage international collaboration are described. Chapter 19 considers some general trends and issues, including the nature of 'quality', common features in quality assurance methods, procedures and agencies, and the growing burden for institutions in responding to external scrutiny. In a concluding chapter, the co-chairs of the conference, draw out some of its major themes.

Each chapter in the collection gives good reasons for establishing particular quality assurance bodies or mechanisms, and for attempting to achieve some international consistency of standards. But some significant dilemmas remain to be more fully addressed. For example, there appears to be some confusion about goals. Should the goal be minimum standards for specific awards, or is it to be exceptional quality? Perhaps this relates to our definition of *higher* education: is it synonymous with *tertiary* education? Where are vocational qualifications located? If there are various forms of tertiary education should they be articulated into a unified qualifications framework, and are the same models of quality assurance appropriate for every type of provision?

Are the methods in use always appropriate? The 'Western' model of quality assurance, based largely on institutional self-study, peer review and site visits, is now internationally widespread and rarely questioned, except for arguments about the link between quality assurance and funding. Is this because it is genuinely functional in every society, or simply because most of the expertise is being disseminated from the 'West'? Effective self-study assumes a tradition of evaluation and self-review which may not always be present. Peer review assumes a willingness to engage in open debate and robust argument without fear or favour, which may be culturally offensive or even politically dangerous in some parts of the world. Where institutions are in fierce competition, or where governments are seeking ideological control, site visits may be open to abuse. Procedures need to be adopted and adapted with care and sensitivity if the quality assurance/accreditation 'movement' is not to be a new form of cultural imperialism.

Finally, we need to be alert to the serious risk — in all societies — that formal agencies and procedures which regulate and control academics and academic standards, may constrain the creativity which is one of higher education's prime purposes. Those who 'manage' the quality assurance process must take care that pressure to conform to quality assurance procedures does not become an end in itself, deflecting attention, energy and resources away from the pursuit of excellence and high academic standards. In this regard, who is going to evaluate the evaluators? Inspect the inspectors? Assure the quality of quality assurance personnel and processes?

The developments reported in this book document the birth of a new quality assurance 'profession'. Like other professions, this is quickly acquiring its own language, culture and mystique; books and journals, conferences and seminars have proliferated; posts are being created, departments and agencies established, careers taking shape. It will be important for this new profession to be seen to practice the self-evaluation and self-assessment it preaches. The International Network which generated the Montreal conference is one useful forum for the fuller exploration of such concerns.

Part I

Regional Perspectives

Chapter 1

Western Europe and North America

Frans van Vught

In this chapter a number of elements of a general model of quality assessment in higher education are presented. These elements are, on the one hand, put in a historical context of quality assessment in medieval universities and, on the other hand, deduced from recent developments in quality assessment in North America and Western Europe. A distinction is made between the intrinsic and the extrinsic values of higher education and the forms of quality assessment related to these values. Recent experiences in the USA, Canada, France, the Netherlands and the United Kingdom are explored, as a basis for the suggested general model.

The Historical Roots of Quality Assessment in Higher Education

From very early days the assessment of the quality of their processes and products has been an important focus of attention for higher education institutions. In this historical attention for quality a certain tension is found which we nowadays still experience and which sometimes appears to be the source of heated debates.

Already in medieval higher education a distinction can be found between two extreme models of quality assessment. Neither of these is of course found in the actual history of European higher education. The models rather point to two crucial dimensions of quality assessment. Referring to their historical backgrounds, I will call one the French model of vesting control in an external authority (Cobban, 1988, p. 124), the other the English model of a self-governing community of fellows.

The French model can be illustrated with the dramatic struggle for autonomy by the University of Paris in the early thirteenth century. The chancellor of the cathedral of Notre Dame, acting as the delegate of the bishop of Paris, represented the then dominating view that the universities should be seen as 'ecclesiastical colonies'. The universities were seen as higher forms of education that were however to be integrated in the ecclesiastical structure and that were to remain under episcopal authority. The chancellor was an external official set above the masters' guild. As such he claimed the authority to grant or to withhold the teaching licence and the right to decide about the content of studies. The masters fought the chancellor's authority. Eventually, after a long and bitter conflict, Pope Gregory IX in his bull *Parens Scientiarum* (1231) ended this dominance of the bishop and the chancellor over the masters' guild (Cobban, 1975, pp. 76–84).

The English model of self-governance has its origins in the medieval universities of Oxford and Cambridge where the masters were completely independent of external jurisdiction. English medieval colleges were sovereign, self-governing communities of fellows. The fellows themselves had the right to remove unsuitable masters, coopt new members, and to judge the quality of their colleagues.

The French medieval model may be considered to be the archetype of quality assessment in terms of accountability. The power to decide what should be studied and who could be allowed to teach at the university was in the hands of an external authority, and the guild masters were accountable to the chancellor for the content of their teaching. The English model is the expression of what we nowadays call quality assessment by means of peer review. The masters decided among themselves what should be taught and who should teach. Together they illustrate two important dimensions of present-day quality assessment in higher education, in which both providing accountability (the French model) and peer review (the English model) are crucial elements.

These two dimensions refer to two subcategories of the general concept of quality that have always played a central role in higher education. Historically, it can be argued that higher education has always had both intrinsic and extrinsic qualities. The intrinsic qualities refer to the ideals of the search for truth and the disinterested pursuit of knowledge. The extrinsic qualities are related to the services higher education institutions provide to society. Higher education institutions have adapted themselves with great flexibility to the changing needs and opportunities in their environment. By combining both intrinsic and extrinsic qualities, they have been able to show a remarkable historical persistence.

The Recent Call of Higher Education Quality Assessment

Since the early 1980s quality has become central to many discussions on higher education. In the United States and Canada debates about the different approaches and instruments with respect to quality assessment have intensified. In the United Kingdom quality became a priority for higher education. In France the Comité National d'Évaluation was established. In the Netherlands an influential policy paper was published in which quality played a major role. In Denmark, Finland, Spain and several other countries the first steps were taken to design a quality assessment system (Neave and van Vught, 1991; van Vught and Westerheijden, 1993).

Various factors can explain this heightened attention to quality. One is the expansion of higher education systems. The rapid growth of the student body and the accompanying increase in the number of fields of study, departments and even whole institutions have triggered questions about the amount and direction of public expenditure for higher education. Another (related) factor lies in the simple fact that the limits of public expenditure have been reached in many countries. Budget cuts and retrenchment operations automatically lead to questions about the relative quality of processes and products. A third factor concerns the transition to technology-based economies which in many countries brings policies to guide student demand towards fields that are perceived to be important for further economic development (Neave, 1986, p. 168).

These developments indicate that during the last ten years or so, it is the extrinsic values of higher education which have driven many governments to policies of quality control. The increasing costs of higher education systems had to be legitimized by clearly definable societal benefits. And for this, mechanisms and procedures of quality assessment were necessary. As a result, new systems of quality assessment and quality control have been (or are being) developed in several countries. But while it may be clear that the extrinsic values of higher education are significant in stimulating these developments, it appears to be difficult to combine governmental goals with the views and characteristics of the higher education institutions themselves.

Experiences in the USA and Canada

As is well-known, in the United States and Canada, the market is the dominant form of coordination in higher education. Competition between institutions is something which is generally accepted, and their organization is somewhat similar to private corporations. There is considerable power at the top of the institution, with a board and a president. Although governmental steering is not completely absent, compared for instance to continental Europe, this influence is limited. The institutions in the United States and Canada are supposed to regulate themselves; if they do not, they will lose resources, students and scholars to their competitors.

In the United States the growing diversity in institutional forms and the initial lack of centrally defined standards led by the late nineteenth century to a level of chaos. If the institutions had not addressed this themselves, strong government intervention would probably have become unavoidable. Because such an intervention was not attractive, the institutions themselves took the initiative to develop two processes of quality assessment (Kells, 1989).

The first process is accreditation. Accreditation of a higher education institution or of a specific study programme within an institution consists of a procedure of self-assessment by the organization seeking accreditation, followed by a visit of a team of external assessors and a final discussion, by a peer-board using pre-existing standards, on the question whether or not to give accreditation. Institutional accreditation is conducted by regional bodies that are controlled by the higher education institutions themselves; specialized accreditation is conducted nationally by profession-controlled bodies.

The second process is the intra-institutional process of systematic review of study programmes. This is undertaken by universities to assess programme quality, to enhance institutional decision-making, and in some cases to provide a basis for the redistribution of marginal resources within the institution (Barak, 1982; Kells and van Vught, 1988; Kells, 1989). Such internal reviews may become an element of the broader accreditation process but this is not necessarily the case.

In Canada, quality assessment in higher education is somewhat differently organized. It does not use the full process of accreditation, but employs two crucial elements of the US approach: self-assessment and the visits by peers as practised by, for example, the technical schools and community colleges in British Columbia and the provincial university of Alberta (Holdaway, 1988).

So, in higher education systems with an emphasis on market coordination and a high level of institutional autonomy (at least compared to some continental European systems) we find an approach to quality assessment which involves a process of self-evaluation (in some cases the assessment is limited to this element); review by peers, usually in the form of a visit by a team of external assessors; and (as in the case of the US) a system of accreditation based on standards that are used to take the decision to give or withhold accreditation.

Developments in Western Europe

Contrary to the United States and Canada, the predominant form of co-ordination in the Western European higher education systems in many countries is still State control, and with the exception of Britain, this has been so for a long period of time. In the centrally controlled continental higher education systems institutional autonomy was rather limited (and in many cases still is), and funding was and is generally provided by the State. However, during the 1970s and the 1980s these systems were confronted with a number of far-reaching changes, most of which can be related in one way or another to a shift in governmental strategies. A major underlying political force was the rise to power of conservative governments in many countries. The so-called 'value-for-money' approach of these governments with respect to the public sector ended the relatively unconditional government funding of higher education. In practice this implied, among other things, that public funding of institutions became linked to performance. As a consequence, the question of how to assess the performance, or quality, of higher education has become a central issue.

A second important development in higher education policy-making in Western Europe is the rise of the governmental strategy of 'self-regulation' (van Vught, 1989; Neave and van Vught, 1991). During the second half of the 1980s, the ministries of education and the higher education institutions, especially in the countries of north-western Europe, have agreed upon the desirability of more self-regulation by the institutions themselves. Several governments have advocated deregulation by central ministries and increased autonomy of, and competitiveness among, the institutions. This move to greater autonomy was generally motivated by governments' wish to stimulate the innovative behaviour of higher education institutions and to stimulate their responsiveness to the perceived needs of the economy and of society. In addition, there was a greater public interest in the quality of study programmes, with an expectation that credible systems of evaluation should be developed.

In response, quality assessment systems were either initiated by the central governmental authorities (as was the case in France) or were negotiated between governments and the leaders of higher education institutions (as was the case in the Netherlands). Together with the United Kingdom, these two countries offer a good overview of recent experiences with quality control in Western Europe.

France

The President of the French Republic and an Act of Parliament brought into being the Comité National d'Évaluation (CNE) in 1985 as a result of the so-called 'Loi Savary'. It was set up in a spirit of concern about the dysfunctions of the traditional and centralized system of quality control: lack of actual autonomy, uniformity, rigidity and bureaucracy (Staropoli, 1992). Given its position in terms of constitutional law, the CNE is a government agency, but since it only reports to the President, it is independent of the Prime Minister, the minister of education and other executive agencies.

The CNE quality assessment procedure consists of institution-wide evaluations and 'horizontal' disciplinary reviews. The evaluations do not assess individuals or specific courses, although where necessary and possible, the CNE makes use of existing evaluations and control reports of other agencies that do examine these and other aspects (such as the Centre for National Scientific Research research laboratories). The tasks of the CNE are not only concerned with quality assessment, but also with judging, quite generally, the results of the contracts established between higher education institutions and the Ministry of Education. Many factual indicators are, therefore, at the basis of the CNE evaluations, including information as diverse as research and finance. Evaluation results are not used directly for making reallocations of funds, though through the contract negotiations and the annual budget negotiations, a firm link with decision-making is established.

The CNE makes institution-wide evaluations of education, research and management, the argument being that research and teaching are interdependent primary activities of higher education institutions. Other aspects of the institution as an environment for teaching and research are also examined.

7

Evaluations are undertaken by invitation and CNE 'tours' all institutions every eight years approximately. Each audit results in a report on the institution, making recommendations to the persons responsible for institutional management. These reports are public. They are sent, among others, to the ministers responsible for the institutions visited, so that they can inform decision-making in the negotiations mentioned above. The whole procedure, from invitation to report, takes about one year (see also Neave, 1991).

The CNE disciplinary reviews consist, first, of self-evaluation reports provided by the institution to be visited. These reports are confidential (and include names of individuals). Second, the CNE, the institution involved and government offices collect statistical data. With those two sources and its own visit to the location, an external peer committee makes qualitative judgments, resulting in a public report. The committees work 'horizontally', reviewing all courses in a broad disciplinary area.

Every year, the CNÉ presents a summary report to the President. In the reports the CNE gives an overview of its institution-wide evaluations. However, no explicit rankings are made of the institutions audited. The character of the reports is sometimes judged to be descriptive rather than analytical (Guin, 1990).

The Netherlands

Following publication of the policy paper *Higher Education: Autonomy and Quality* (1985), the relationship between the Ministry of Education and Science and the higher education institutions in the Netherlands was restructured. In exchange for a greater degree of financial and managerial autonomy, the institutions would prove to society (in fact, to the government) that they delivered quality education. Originally, the government intended this evaluation to be executed by the Inspectorate for Higher Education (IHO). In subsequent discussions the umbrella organizations of the higher education institutions, the Association of Cooperating Universities in the Netherlands (VSNU) and the Council for non-university higher education institutions (HBO), took that responsibility on themselves. The IHO was bypassed through that compromise and was largely left with the task of 'meta-evaluation': evaluation of the evaluations, and evaluation of the follow up on assessment results by the higher education institutions. The evaluation of the 1988 VSNU pilot project led to some adjustments and its quality assessment activity became operational in 1989. In 1990 the HBO Council started a procedure in the non-university sector that, although not completely following to the VSNU approach, is based on the same basic principles.

For reasons of brevity this chapter concentrates on the VSNU system. The focal point is the visiting committee that reviews all study programmes in a given area of knowledge in the country; the approach is by disciplinary fields, rather than institutional. In a fixed six-year cycle, in principle all study programmes are covered. In preparation for the visiting committee, each participating study programme is required to write a self-evaluation. As this aims not only to prepare the faculty for the visiting committee, but also to stimulate internal quality management (Vroeijenstijn and Acherman 1990), the content of the self-evaluation is not completely predetermined: the faculties and departments to be evaluated can stress points which are important to them. However, for reasons of comparability, a fixed format is given by the VSNU checklist (VSNU, 1990). The self-studies of all participating study programmes are collected by the visiting committee before it starts on its 'tour' of the country.

The visiting committees consist of about seven members, including at least one foreign expert in the field. Members are proposed by the collective deans of the participating faculties and nominated by the board of the VSNU. The committee visits each study programme for, normally, two or two and a half days. During this period the committee speaks with representatives of all interest groups in the faculty, including students. To enable non-selected voices to be heard, an 'open hour' is part of the procedure. Subjects for the talks are taken from the self-evaluation, from the committee's prior visits and other (usually considerable) knowledge of the field and the faculty, and whatever else comes up during the visit. At the end of the visit, the chair gives an oral, temporary judgment about the quality of the study programme. Based on the written version of this judgment and (factual) corrections from the study programmes, the committee then writes its final report. The report usually contains a general section stating problems, outlooks, expectations and recommendations pertaining to all of the field, and chapters about the individual study programmes. The recommendations in the report supposedly lead to improvements in the study programmes, together with the measures taken based on the self-evaluations in anticipation of the site visit.

As a result of the agreements of 1986, the Ministry of Education and Science has not taken any action on the basis of the visiting committees' judgments. It was argued then that the introduction of the system should not be hampered by direct consequences for decision-making and funding. Direct links to funding and other aspects of government decision-making would lead only too easily to strategic behaviour on the part of the higher education institutions, which would undermine the quality assessment system completely.

The United Kingdom

In the United Kingdom, two models of quality management have been developed since the enlargement of government influence over higher education in the 1960s. The first model applied to the non-university sector — the polytechnics and colleges. Much later, quality assessment was extended to university higher education and there are now new arrangements with respect to quality assessment as a result of the 1991 White Paper *Higher Education: A New Framework*, formalized in the *Further and Higher Education Act* of 1992.

From the first half of the 1960s non-university higher education in the UK was under the aegis of the CNAA, the Council of National Academic Awards (Brennan, 1990). As in other countries, quality in this sector was also controlled by Her Majesty's Inspectorate (HMI), which continued to operate, with its own responsibilities and methods, alongside the new CNAA. The main characterizing element of HMI procedures was classroom observation.

The CNAA, a government-initiated body, was independent: it obtained its own Royal Charter in 1964. It was a degree-awarding body, giving out degrees of a professedly equal level to those of universities. The CNAA validated proposed courses in colleges and polytechnics *ex ante* and reviewed them quinquennially. Institutions were visited by specialist panels consisting of peers, i.e., academics working in the same area of knowledge but from other higher education institutions (colleges, polytechnics and universities), plus, if applicable, representatives of the relevant profession or industry. These committees based their visit on detailed written information regarding the structure and content of the course, ways and methods of teaching and student assessment, and available resources (research and teaching qualifications of the staff members who were expected to become involved, physical equipment, etc.). In the cases of non-approval by the panel a new round, based on an amended proposal, would start.

This peer review of courses was complemented by a, usually quinquennial, review of the institution's own operational (i.e., not just existing on paper) mechanisms for assuring the level of its courses. From 1988, the CNAA accredited a number of polytechnics allowing then to validate their own courses (undergraduate and postgraduate degree level), though the Council continued its monitoring of their institutional quality management procedures. By taking account of the institution's goals and aims the CNAA and the public sector funding organization (the Polytechnics and Colleges Funding Council) tried to liberalize the evaluation culture developing in the 1980s, which was becoming more and more government-centred.

In 1992, the binary system in the UK was abolished and the polytechnics became universities. The CNAA ceased to exist, with its activities ending more or less with the academic year 1991–2. The turning points in quality management for British universities were two reports in the mid-1980s: the Reynolds report to the Universities' Grants Committee (UGC) and the Jarratt report to the Committee of Vice Chancellors and Principals (CVCP). In the Reynolds report criteria were laid down for internal quality management systems which all universities would be required to introduce in the following years. The Jarratt report was the focal point for the discussion of performance indicators and their role in quality-based funding.

The Academic Audit Unit (AAU) was introduced in 1990–1 by the CVCP, the umbrella organization of the universities, reputedly to counter the threat of Her Majesty's Inspectorate (HMI) to extend its control to the universities (Young, 1990). Before this, each university individually took care of its own quality control, and the external, comparative aspect in this system consisted largely of external examiners. Views on the effectiveness of external examiners in terms of quality assessment differ, and this approach was judged to be an insufficient mechanism for providing accountability towards society in general and to the government in particular. The AAU had to fill this gap.

The AAU activities were a form of 'meta-evaluation': it did not evaluate the quality of higher education, but the quality of the institution's evaluation methods. The core procedure consisted of an on-site visit by an audit team. The teams consisted of academics, as a rule two or three persons. The choice of institutions to visit resulted from 'negotiated invitation'. In preparation for its (usually three-day) visit the audit team received written information from the university on the quality assessment systems it had, plus — if requested — a small number of examples of the application of these systems. The AAU had a checklist based on good practice against which to assess an institution's own mechanisms. From this documentation together with the information gathered during the on-site visit the audit team drafted a short report for the university as a whole and, if necessary, confidential reports on 'sensitive issues' to the Vice-Chancellor. Following the institution's comments on this draft, a final version of the official report was prepared. The AAU did not itself publish the report, but the university was encouraged to do so.

The changes following the 1991 White Paper have led to profound organizational restructuring at the intermediate level between the individual institutions and the Department for Education. First, the collective of heads of higher education institutions established the Higher Education Quality Council (HEQC) with a Division of Quality Audit, into which the AAU has been subsumed, together with the past work of the CNAA in supporting and enhancing quality. Second, the former funding councils (the Universities Funding Council and the Polytechnics and Colleges Funding Council) have been transformed into three new funding councils, one for England, one for Wales and one for Scotland. These have each set up Quality Assessment Committees to assist them in making funding decisions based on the quality of teaching in the separate institutions (see also Chapter 11).

The White Paper has also introduced very specific meanings for the following terms in the British context:

- *quality control*: 'mechanisms within institutions for maintaining and enhancing the quality of their provisions';
- *quality audit*: 'external scrutiny aimed at providing guarantees that institutions have suitable quality control mechanisms in place' (this is the responsibility of the HEQC); and
- *quality assessment*: 'external review of, and judgments about, the quality of teaching and learning in institutions' (this is the responsibility of the funding councils).

Higher education institutions are thus being audited by one agency, and assessed by another. The quality audits by the HEQC closely resemble the basic principles of the AAU: an investigation of the quality control mechanisms and policies present in the individual institutions by a small team of external experts, including *in loco* audit trails to examine the practice of quality control.

Although there are some differences in the approaches of three Funding Councils (for example, the Scottish Funding Council taking a slightly more explicitly developmental and quality improvement oriented stance than the English one), on a general level they are fairly similar. Basically, the faculties are asked to provide information about themselves in writing on a limited number of indicators, and on their programmes, resulting in a claim for 'excellent' or 'satisfactory' quality of teaching. The funding councils assemble small visiting committees from a pool of experts (primarily disciplinary peers), to assess and visit all institutions with a *prima facie* case for excellence, all those where — based on information available to the funding council — weaknesses may be encountered, and a sample of other institutions. The same visiting committee may visit several institutions but no effort is made to set up a nationwide system of comparisons. The committees' judgments are summarized as 'excellent', 'satisfactory' or 'unsatisfactory' (in Scotland, there is a four-point scale). In what way, through which 'formula' (if any), the judgments inform the funding decisions remains controversial. There are concerns about overlap between the practices of quality audit and quality assessment, and the extent to which an audit trail into the practice of quality control in a faculty closely resembles the quality assessment of that same faculty.

A General Model of Higher Education Quality Assessment

Overlooking the experiences with quality assessment systems both in the USA and Canada, and in the western European countries just mentioned, it can be argued that each system has its own characteristics, but that there are a number of similar elements that can be combined into the core of a general higher education quality assessment system.

Crucial to such a general model is the assumption that quality assessment in higher education should have both an intrinsic and an extrinsic dimension. In any sensible system both the traditional English model of a review by peers and the historical French model of providing accountability to external constituencies should be incorporated. Focusing on only one of these two models leads to a risky overestimation of specific functions and practices of higher education institutions. A quality control system which only takes place by means of collegial peer review without any reference to the needs outside the system, runs the risk of isolation of the institutions from the rest of society (and thus the danger of the denial of legitimacy of their existence). A quality control system which is limited only to providing accountability to external authorities denies some of the basic organizational characteristics of higher education institutions and therefore runs the risk of not being taken seriously by the academic experts.

What then could be common elements of a general model of higher education quality assessment? A first element concerns the managing agent (or agents). Such an agent should be independent and have responsibility at a meta-level. The meta-level agent should be the coordinator of the quality assessment system, acting independently from government politics and policies and not having the task of imposing upon institutions an approach that the government deems to be necessary. The meta-level agent should preferably have some legal basis. Its coordinating task should include (after consultation with the institutions) the formulation of procedures and formats that can be used by the institutions. In these procedures, consistent statistical information can be indicated as highly relevant. Experiences in Western Europe shows that this meta-level role is of great importance to obtain acceptance of the system. The AAU in the United Kingdom neither inspected courses nor programmes, nor did it validate courses. It only monitored and commented on the mechanisms by which the institutions themselves assured the quality of the programmes they offer. Similarly, in the procedures used by the CNAA, the institutions were encouraged to undertake their own quality review processes. While the CNAA retained responsibility for the final approval of the courses leading to its awards, the initial quality assessment exercise concerned the institution's capacity to identify its own strengths and weaknesses and to improve its quality. In the new British system, two meta-level agents exist, namely the Higher Education Quality Council, 'owned' by the collective universities, and the funding councils, which are tied more closely to government. The VSNU in the Netherlands follows a similar strategy, with emphasis on the institution's self-evaluation and the visit by peers. The VSNU itself only operates as the coordinator of the system.

A second common element which may be deduced from both the North American and the Western European experiences, is that any quality assessment system must be based on self-evaluation (or self-study, self-assessment). It is often argued in literature on higher education that, in order for academics to accept and implement changes, they must trust and 'own' the process in which problems are defined and solutions are designed. This is certainly also the case in quality assessment. Only if the academics accept quality assessment as their own activity, will the system be successful, thus self-evaluation is a crucial mechanism. And in this self-evaluation process, consultation with outside actors (employers, alumni) is of great importance.

A third common element certainly appears to be the mechanism of peer review and especially one or more site visits by external experts. It is essential that these external experts should be accepted by the institution to be visited as unbiased specialists in the field. They can come from many constituencies (including employers' organizations, industry and professional bodies) and, depending on the nature of the visit (review of content and level of a specific study programme, or management audit at the institutional level), they will need to have specific backgrounds (academic expertise, managerial experience, etc.). The externals should visit the institution (or faculty/department) for a period of a few days, during which they can discuss the self-evaluation report and any plans for future innovations. The visitors can also take the opportunity to interview staff, students, administrators and (if possible) alumni. This element appears to be used successfully in both North America and Western Europe. In the USA and Canada a visit by peers always has been a crucial aspect of the various assessment systems. In the UK the CNAA emphasized the visit by a committee of peers. The Academic Audit Unit saw the visit as an intense and concentrated activity (Williams, 1991, pp. 7–8). The procedures developed following the recent changes in British higher education continue this emphasis: although for reasons of economy the funding councils abstain from visits to all faculties, all those whose quality is claimed or expected to deviate from the average will be visited, plus a sample of the 'satisfactory' ones. In France the Comité National d'Évaluation organizes at least two visits to each university being reviewed. In the Netherlands a team of external experts visits each programme site of a specific discipline.

A fourth element of a general model of quality assessment concerns the reporting of the results of, and experience with, the methods used. Regarding this, it may first of all be pointed out that some form of reporting the conclusions of the peer review team is very useful. Such a report should not have the function of judging or ranking the institutions or programmes that have been visited. It rather should have as its main objective to help the institutions and study programmes to improve their levels of quality. A crucial phase in the reporting process therefore is the opportunity for the institutions and units that have been visited to comment on a draft version of the report and to formulate counter-arguments if necessary. And, in the final version of the report higher education institutions should be able to indicate possible disagreements with the peer review team.

Reporting the results of the quality assessment processes is an important mechanism in the process of providing accountability to external constituencies. However, there appear to be various ways of offering such a report and each has its specific advantages and disadvantages. One way is to publish the complete report and, by so doing, offer it to all those who might be interested. The advantage of such an approach is that each constituency can immediately and clearly find out what the outcomes of an assessment have been and how these outcomes relate to their norms and criteria. A disadvantage is that this may severely limit the commitment of those who are visited to engage in open discussions with the peer review team, simply because they fear the effects of their frankness when the results of the review are published. A second way is to offer the detailed individual reports only to the institutions visited and to guarantee confidentiality. To the external constituencies (and to society at large) a general summary of the report can be presented, which may be used as a mechanism for providing accountability. The advantage of this approach is that the commitment of those who are visited will be high. The disadvantage is that some external constituencies may not be satisfied with only a summary of the report, fearing that information is being withheld from them.

In the USA and Canada, reports are usually kept confidential. In France, the institutional self-evaluations are kept confidential, while the CNE report by the external experts is public. In the Netherlands, although in the pilot phase the external visitors' reports on the individual study programmes were kept confidential, since the system has been fully implemented they have been made public. The argument for doing so is the accountability objective. The British Academic Audit Unit's reports were intended to provide an accurate account of institutions' quality assurance mechanisms, drawing attention to good and bad practice. Written primarily for the institution and not published by the Academic Audit Unit itself, it was left to the institution to decide what publicity to give to the final report, although it was assumed that this would 'find its way into the public domain accompanied by a commentary prepared by the university' (Williams, 1991). UK reports are now published.

A final common element of a general model of quality assessment concerns the possible relationship between the outcomes of a quality review and (governmental) decisions about the *funding* of higher education activities. Based on the experience of quality assessment especially in Western Europe so far, it is argued here that a direct, rigid relationship between quality review reports and funding decisions should not be established. Any such relationship implies that the quality judgments are the only input into the funding process, and that this moreover, is a simple linear function of the quality judgment: 'good' education means x extra money, and 'bad' education means x money less. Such an 'automatic' direct relationship will probably harm the operation of a quality assessment system. All the more so as funding decisions presently tend to be cutbacks (negative sanctions) rather than incentives (positive sanctions). The danger of this is that it may lead to a compliance culture, the only aim of which will be to appear to meet the criteria formulated, irrespective of whether those criteria are appropriate in the context of specific institutions. In such a rigid relationship, academics and institutions will distrust the external review teams and they will produce self-evaluation studies which comply with perceived criteria but with little real interest. Relating a system of rigid and direct rewards and sanctions to the delicate mechanisms of quality assessment may have a very negative effect on the operation of the system. In France, the CNE has understood these dangers. The Committee evaluations are not intended to impact on state subventions to the institutions. The new procedures for quality assessment in the United Kingdom also do not imply a direct relationship between quality management and funding on a large scale, since the amounts of money affected by the funding councils' judgments seem to be fairly marginal for the moment, thereby mitigating any possible negative effect. The quality audits of the HEQC as it continues the role of the AAU, have no direct link to funding either.

The above does not imply that an indirect, non-automatic relationship between quality management and funding decisions should also be rejected. On the contrary, as the experiences in the USA and Canada as well as the new approaches in France and the United Kingdom show, such an indirect relationship, where quality judgments are one — but not the only one — of the inputs into the policy processes leading to funding decisions, could very well be part of the general model of quality assessment suggested here. An indirect relationship would imply that national governments will only provide the necessary financial means to higher education institutions if these institutions (and the various units within these institutions) can show that they have submitted themselves to at least one external judgment which is an accepted part of the general quality assessment system. The decision on institutional funding thus depends on willingness to submit to outside review, but it should be left to the discretion of the institutions to decide for themselves their reactions to the outcomes of the quality assessment. Whether the funds provided by government are used to reward programmes that are judged to be of good quality, or to help programmes that receive a negative evaluation by an external review team, should be the decision of the higher education institution itself.

The elements presented here (touching upon the meta-level role of managing agent(s), upon self-evaluation, upon peer review and site visits, upon the degree of confidentiality of reporting, and upon the relationship between quality review outcomes and funding) together form the core of what could be called a general model of higher education quality assessment. In this model both the intrinsic and the extrinsic values of higher education are addressed, combining the two traditional approaches to quality assessment and relating present-day experiences to their historical roots.

References

BARAK, R.J. (1982) *Program Review in Higher Education*, National Center for Higher Education Management Systems, Boulder, Colorado.

BRENNAN, J. (1990) 'Quality assessment in the public sector in Great Britain', in GOEDEGEBUURE, L.C.J., MAASSEN, P.A.M. and WESTERHEIJDEN, D.F. (Eds) *Peer Review and Performance Indicators*, Utrecht, Lemma.

COBBAN, A.B. (1975) *The Medieval Universities, their Development and Organisation*, London, Methuen and Co.

COBBAN, A.B. (1988) *The Medieval English Universities: Oxford and Cambridge to C. 1500*, Berkeley, University of California Press.

GUIN, J. (1990) 'The reawakening of higher education in France', *European Journal of Education*, 25.

HOLDAWAY, E.A. (1988) 'Institutional self-study and the improvement of quality', in KELLS, H.R. and VAN VUGHT, F.A. (Eds) *Self-Regulation, Self-Study and Program Review in Higher Education*, Utrecht, Lemma.

KELLS, H.R. (1989) 'University self-regulation in Europe, the need for an integrated system of program review', *European Journal of Education*, 24.

KELLS, H.R. and VAN VUGHT, F.A. (Eds) (1988) *Self-Regulation, Self-Study and Program Review in Higher Education*, Utrecht, Lemma.

NEAVE, G. (1986) 'The all-seeing eye of the prince in Western Europe', in MOODIE, G.C. (Ed) *Standards and Criteria in Higher Education*, Guildford, NFER-Nelson.

NEAVE, G. and VAN VUGHT, F.A. (Eds) (1991) *Prometheus Bound, the Changing Relationship between Government and Higher Education in Western Europe*, London, Pergamon.

NEAVE, M. (1991) *Models of Quality Assessment in Europe*, London, CNAA Discussion Paper 6.

STAROPOLI, A. (1992) 'The French Comité National d'Evaluation', in CRAFT, A. (Ed) *Quality Assurance in Higher Education*, London, Falmer Press.

VSNU (1990) *Guide for External Program Review*, Utrecht.

VROEIJENSTIJN, T.I. and ACHERMAN, H. (1990) 'Control oriented versus improvement oriented quality assessment', in GOEDEGEBUURE, L.C.J., MAASSEN, P.A.M. and WESTERHEIJDEN, D.F. (Eds) *Peer Review and Performance Indicators*, Utrecht, Lemma.

VUGHT, VAN F.A. (Ed) (1989) *Governmental Strategies and Innovation in Higher Education*, London, Jessica Kingsley.

VUGHT, VAN F.A. and WESTERHEIJDEN, D.F. (1993) *Quality Management and Quality Assurance in European Higher Education*, Brussels, European Communities.

WILLIAMS, P.R. (1991) *The CVCP Academic Audit Unit*, Birmingham.

YOUNG, D. (1990) 'The academic audit unit, an organisation for university quality management', in GOEDEGEBUURE, L.C.J., MAASSEN, P.A.M. and WESTERHEIJDEN, D.F. (Eds) *Peer Review and Performance Indicators*, Utrecht, Lemma.

Chapter 2

Latin America

Hernan Ayarza

This chapter provides an overview of university accreditation in the countries of Latin America, where higher education is facing the basic problem of improving and assuring academic quality. It draws on papers presented at an international seminar held in Santiago, Chile.

University Development in Latin America

Latin American universities emerged at the turn of the sixteenth century. Modelled after the Salamanca University in Spain, their purpose was to train personnel in the service of Church and State, and their teaching methodology was largely expository. Following independence, national universities in each Latin American country became more functional and secular and were state-run. They were increasingly oriented to teaching for the professions such as law, medicine and engineering, and came closer to the French model. Later, rationalism and the development of natural sciences modified teaching approaches although they remained essentially expository and memory-based and the main mission of the university was still to educate the cadres of the ruling and political élite. During this century, the University of Córdoba Movement in Argentina in 1918 began the process of reform towards university autonomy from the State government. And in the 1960s, social changes and the access to university of new social groups and of women, led to substantial shifts.

As of then, a qualitative change occurred in teaching. It became more comprehensive and research-oriented, and more linked to national reality. Students were offered a more balanced education, not solely centered on professional training, and with greater emphasis on the social and cultural.

Latin American countries are now bent upon an intense process of social development and economic growth — with marked openness towards the rest of the world. This calls for effective use of all their resources, particularly their national scientific and technological capacity, since the latter is indispensable for selecting, adapting and transferring appropriate technologies from abroad, and for developing countries' own technology.

18

It is currently believed that the incorporation of knowledge into production — 'technical progress' — involving education, training, and scientific and technological innovation, is one of the most important factors in economic development. Over 50 per cent of the growth achieved by developed countries is attributed to this (Sáez, 1984); yet even in the more advanced Latin American countries this factor accounts for less than 30 per cent of growth. Almost all of Latin America's national scientific and technological capacity resides in its universities. Through their educational and research activities and their support for productive development, in the form of training, technical assistance and transfer of technology, the universities therefore represent a very significant resource in the pursuit of rapid development. Yet they in turn require huge resources from society in general and from the State in particular. So as not to betray public faith and expectations, efficient and effective use must be made of these resources. Thus it is their importance in solving national social problems, their role as the main generators of useful knowledge for national development and their responsibility in training educated professionals and citizens with technical, political and social skills, which explains the growing concern for the evaluation and accreditation of Latin American higher education institutions.

One of the most significant factors affecting the quality of universities is the wide institutional diversity recently brought about by the large number of private higher education institutions incorporated into the system — institutions that are horizontally and vertically very differentiated. The heterogeneity this has produced in post-secondary education has heightened concerns about the lack of accreditation mechanisms and of adequate and reliable information about educational quality within this new context.

Current Experience in University Accreditation

Conceptual Framework

If the university is regarded as an institution whose mission, activities and results should ensure the harmonious and comprehensive development of man and society, it should respond and be accountable to the national community that surrounds and sustains it. This necessarily means that the evaluation of higher education institutions should take into account their social, economic and educational relevance, with a view to verifying the extent to which they fulfil their commitment to society.

University evaluation in Latin America is not common practice, and there is relatively little experience with regard to well-established policies, systems or mechanisms, based on recognized, independent and objective criteria, against which universities and faculties can review their work, their results and their academics in a systematic and rigorous way.

In virtually all countries of the region there are formal procedures for granting official recognition to the operation of a new university, although these may differ in the nature and degree of requirements. But once legally established, the universities enjoy full autonomy. They alone are responsible for granting academic and professional degrees, according to their own academic standards. There are no permanent procedures for regular evaluation and accreditation, except in Colombia and Brazil, where they have not been entirely successful.

Senior managers and professors in the university systems are generally in favour of establishing some sort of evaluatory process, believing that it has the potential to contribute a better understanding of an institution's shortcomings and strengths. But many university teachers are resisting the changes, viewing these processes as control mechanisms with possible implications for academic careers and tenure, and for academic freedom.

Brunner (1991) suggests that the crisis affecting higher education systems in Latin America is essentially due to their being unable to adapt to new circumstances and the challenges required by rapid social development and growth, which call for changes in the way they conceive of their organization and their relationship with the State. The inadequacy of the traditional structure of relations between higher education systems, society and governments has had a paralyzing effect on their development. For this reason, it is proposed to introduce a new social contract, based on an evaluation relationship with the State, on diversifying sources of income and on a differentiated handling of State resources in terms of agreed objectives and goals.

The Latin American model is complex because of the factors within each country that condition the methods, procedures and mechanisms in use (CINDA, 1991). Accreditation, evaluation and regulation of universities are very closely interrelated, but it is possible to identify three distinct phases.

- 'Recognition' is the official authorization of an institution to begin its academic activities;
- 'Systematic follow-up' is undertaken by some legally established or jointly agreed modality to verify its capacity to implement its educational goals successfully; once this verification is completed, the institution may obtain full autonomy; and
- 'Accreditation', and the attendant self-evaluation on which it is based, is a systematic and ongoing process by which an external agency confirms the academic quality of an institution.

The accreditation model in Latin America is largely based on the system of voluntary self-regulation developed by the various university associations in the United States and modified to suit the diverse realities of the region. It involves verification of the results of an institution's self-study or self-evaluation, and is undertaken by an external body, according to established standards, which the universities that are voluntarily incorporated into the system, know and agree to comply with. Although the process is not developed to the same extent in all countries, the self-evaluation associated with the accreditation of institutions or programs is considered to be an essential element in improving quality. Accreditation is generally regarded as an effective element in ensuring recognition and public faith, as well as a powerful factor in obtaining access to public or private funding in a fairer and more objective way.

Although experience in Latin American countries is quite recent, there is a high degree of consensus regarding the importance and urgency of establishing strong evaluation and accreditation systems. The following account of the situation in several different countries shows that more experience exists than is generally assumed. In some countries it has evolved over several years, and it seems likely that there will soon be formal quality assurance systems in most of the region. Hopefully, this will contribute to improving higher education and to greater recognition and legitimacy for university institutions, and will also facilitate the recognition of degrees and student and professional exchanges at regional and national level.

In 1991, CINDA (Centro Interuniverseritario de Desarrollo, based in Chile) organized a seminar on 'Accreditation in Latin American and Caribbean Universities'. The papers presented at that seminar have provided the basis for this overview of accreditation in the Caribbean, Mexico and South America. Each case is described from the standpoint of higher education development in the respective country.

Caribbean Countries

Some of the Caribbean countries are English-speaking, with a major cultural influence from the British Commonwealth. Others are Spanish-speaking with strong cultural ties and similarities with Latin America. Then, there is Haiti and other French-speaking countries, and lastly, Puerto Rico, which, although hispanic in origin, has an educational system influenced by the United States.

In 1988, the Steering Committee of the Ministers of Education (SCME) of CARICOM began a study on the equivalence of academic credentials in the region. Subsequently, in 1990, the regional strategy was broadened to assist member countries to develop the coordination and accreditation of their higher education institutions and programs, foreshadowing the establishment of a common accreditation system in the future. Although a formal accreditation system is still lacking, there is consensus that once established, it will have a significant impact on all Caribbean higher education.

Trinidad and Tobago

Higher education in Trinidad and Tobago, as well as in the other twelve Caribbean Community (CARICOM) member countries, follows the British model (Ashton, 1991). There are only two universities — the University of the West Indies (UWI), in Jamaica, and the University of Guyana, which is regional in nature, with campuses in Trinidad and Tobago and in Barbados. There is also the College of Arts, Science and Technology (CAST) in Jamaica, offering advanced school-level technology programs.

In 1979, the Committee on the Recognition of Degrees (CORD) was created in Trinidad and Tobago to advise the government on the recognition of foreign degrees, accreditation and on the quality of post-secondary education offered in the country. New legislation on community colleges is being considered, including an autonomous accreditation mechanism, that will affect all private and public institutions.

The Dominican Republic

The most salient features of the Dominican higher education system have been its extraordinary quantitative expansion and the extensive participation by the private sector over the past thirty years (de Miguel Lopez, 1991). That the only condition for the foundation of private higher education institutions, established by legislation in 1966 and 1967, is 'respect for public order' to some extent explains their number.

The great competition between universities, and the need for differentiation and to improve quality, led a group of deans in 1981 to found the Asociación Dominicana de Rectores de Universidades (ADRU). One of their most important initiatives was to create the Asociación Dominicana para el Autoestudio y la Acreditación (ADAA), whose main purpose is to promote the maintenance and improvement of higher education quality, through self-study and accreditation of their member institutions. For this, their organization received advisory assistance from the Middle States Association of Colleges and Schools of the United States. The impact of ADAA in the Dominican university milieu is generally regarded as positive, and may be a useful model for other countries of the continent.

Mexico

In Mexico there is no accreditation system that periodically and systematically seeks to ensure that higher education institutions are fulfilling their teaching, research and cultural diffusion roles under previously established conditions of quality, since expansion to meet the growing demand for post-secondary education has taken precedence (Chapela, 1991). More recently the Mexican higher education system has moved from a stage of quantitative growth in student enrolment, towards an emphasis on qualitative improvements.

In 1989, the Comisión Nacional de Evaluación de la Educación Superior (CONAEVA) was created. Its purpose is to conceive of, and coordinate, the evaluation of higher education in the entire country, to give continuity and permanence to the evaluation process and to propose criteria and standards of quality for the roles and tasks of university institutions. In May 1990, CONAEVA made specific recommendations regarding evaluation. First, universities should prepare and deliver pertinent information, by means of a questionnaire prepared by CONAEVA. Second, they should receive visits by commissions of experts from the various academic areas, for the qualitative evaluation of teaching at undergraduate, postgraduate and research levels.

However by the end of 1991, only two institutions had undertaken their internal or self-evaluation, which illustrates the difficulty of establishing an evaluatory system where a culture of evaluation is lacking. Nevertheless, what is important is that the process has begun and that, even amongst those who are most critical discussion focuses on its modalities and secondary aspects. Visits by peer committees have also begun: these act as a collegiate body composed of nine academics of renowned prestige and one specialist from the productive sector.

The establishment of a national accreditation system is foreseeable in the medium-term. The participation of institutions grouped under the Asociación Nacional de Universidades e Instituciones de Educación Superior (ANUIES) is anticipated, although it is possible there may be different arrangements for each group of institutions in the Association, that is, the universities, technical institutes and teacher training colleges.

South America

In South America, Brazil, Colombia and Chile have accreditation systems with wide coverage operating on a regular basis, although differing in characteristics and modalities. Elsewhere projects are being implemented, and a favourable attitude is evident on the part of their educational authorities. All are State-run, and systematic activities are underway for improving them, taking account of the shortcomings detected in practice.

Brazil
Brazil's concern about higher education and its relationship with national development dates back to the 1930s (Neiva, 1991). However, it is only since the 1970s that proposals and ideas on evaluation have been presented. This is intended to be the basis for recognition and accreditation of new institutions and programs; as a mechanism for adjustments to higher education expansion; and as a social instrument for reviewing and controlling the quality of teaching and research.

The higher education system in Brazil depends on the Ministry of Education, which exerts its authority by means of the Federal Education Council (CFE). In 1975, and then again in 1984, the Ministry established some control requirements for planning and decision-making in relation to new establishments and courses. Recognition of undergraduate programs is authorized once the first cohort graduates, and this authorization must be renewed every five years. In 1986, the minister introduced the notion of internal and external evaluation of undergraduate institutions, but nothing was formalized about evaluation processes or procedures.

Recently, following heavy criticism of higher education and faced with a serious economic and financial crisis, the State has adopted a new policy based on two strategic courses of action — one aimed at identifying the main problems and the other at providing technical and financial support for research projects on methodology and for the internal and external evaluation of undergraduate provision. This has constituted the basis of the so-called 'National Evaluation Program', whose implementation in macroscopic perspective, has encountered various problems. The main difficulties arise from the huge diversity of programs, making action by a centralized body (in this case the CFE) virtually impossible. There is a lack of uniformity in the indicators used, and a dearth of specialized personnel within the institutions to undertake the design, execution and analysis required by a self-evaluation system. Experiences in methodical voluntary evaluation are few and far between.

At present, the attempts at undergraduate accreditation are primarily aimed at establishing criteria for resource allocation and at determining some control indicators such as professor–student ratios, cost of teaching, etc. It is argued that new legislation regulating university autonomy should establish more effective procedures for evaluating institutional quality and performance. The successful experience of CAPES, the organization for postgraduate program evaluation, is frequently used as a reference (de Rezende Martins, 1991). However, this model does not appear to be easily transferable to undergraduate education since it is only concerned with advanced programs in a small number of institutions with reasonable standards of quality.

Bolivia

Universities in Bolivia are part of a national body called the Universidad Boliviana, whose executive committee prepared a Program of University Self-improvement, Methodologies and Conceptual Decisions, which considers institutional evaluation to be the basis for qualitative institutional change (Universidad Boliviana, 1991). This program sets out strategies to begin to initiate an institutional evaluation system, to coordinate and advise on its implementation in universities, and to systematize the resulting information. This process is at an early stage, and no results are yet available.

Colombia

The Colombian experience is one of the most extensive and long-standing, although this does not exempt it from controversy (Galarza, 1991). The Instituto Colombiano de Fomento at la Educación Superior (ICFES) is the official body in charge of supervising the national higher education system (Martinez, 1991). ICFES was created in 1968 as an auxiliary body of the Ministry of Education to supervise the quality of higher education and to provide technical, economic and administrative assistance to institutions. A short time later, its role as promoter virtually disappeared, and it took on the role of State institution devoted to controlling all university activities — from the creation of programs and cost of enrolment, to the approval of statutes within each institution. By 1991, it was physically impossible for ICFES to control all 252 Colombian institutions and their 2,000 different programs. Its control system is incongruent with the times and with the conception of the modern university.

Reform of the legislation regulating higher education and a restructuring of ICFES was recently proposed, with total autonomy for the production of knowledge, its validation and dissemination. But, given that education is considered a public service, the State reserves the right of control. Proposals include a user information system and institutional accreditation based on higher education quality indicators, as part of a national university evaluation system.

The creation of new private universities depends upon ICFES, which confers juridical status upon them. To begin functioning, they also require approval of their study programs. Public institutions are created by decision of a governmental authority, but for their study programs they too must have ICFES approval. Program approval is temporary, initially for a five-year period, but can become permanent over time. The institutions themselves must submit a self-evaluation and the Asociación Combaniana de Universidades (ASCUN) plays an active role in promoting institutional self-evaluation among its members. ICFES itself organizes periodic inspection by review committees.

Venezuela

Venezuela has both postgraduate and undergraduate evaluation procedures under the auspices of the Consejo Nacional de Universidades (CINDA, 1991). This is a state body, created by law, empowered to grant operating licenses to new, experimental higher education institutions, and to follow them up until the graduation of the first cohort of students. Summative evaluations are then undertaken. The institutions evaluated must re-register every five years, maintaining their status as experimental institutions until they reach full autonomy. For this, account is taken of their academic capacity, assessed in terms of their educational plan, professors, their contractual condition and their academic level. This process evolves without explicit accreditation by any external body.

Chile

Since 1982, Chilean higher education has changed radically. From eight consolidated universities each with great disciplinary and specialization coverage, the system has expanded to a very large number of institutions widely differing in scope. Two parallel systems of 'examination' and 'accreditation' now coexist in the creation and initial supervision of new institutions, differing in mechanisms and criteria.

The examination system was established by law in 1981, whereby new institutions had to submit to examination by a traditional university, according to an agreement signed between both (Albornoz, 1991; Alonso, 1991). Examination involves approval or modification by the examining university of the study plans and programs of the new institution according to the former's own curricular criteria, and assessment of the academic achievement of the student body from the new institution. Once the requirements have been met, the new university obtains official recognition and full autonomy, without any subsequent evaluation.

The Organic Constitutional Law on Teaching (LODE) of 1990 introduced accreditation as a new procedure for officially recognizing new higher education institutions (Covarrubias, 1991), although institutions which at that time were under the examination system could choose to remain in it. Accreditation is broader in scope than examination, and is undertaken by the Higher Education Council, a body constituted by the 1990 Law, which has contributed to greater institutional ordering. The institution freely and independently presents itself to the Council, which then verifies the institution's teaching programs, teaching techniques, research proposals, physical aspects and infrastructure, and economic and financial resources, in relation to the academic and professional degrees it offers. At the end of the process, Council accreditation confers full academic autonomy, without any subsequent evaluation.

Although only recently introduced, and although limited in scope and coverage, these developments are generally believed to be a very important step towards the qualitative and quantitative improvement of the Chilean higher education system. However, the concept of regulation, evaluation or accreditation is still associated primarily with new, private institutions, and it is currently argued that it is not appropriate or advisable to exempt the long-standing, traditional public or state-subsidized private institutions from such a process, given that their impact is far greater than that of the new private institutions. (For a fuller account of the developments in Chile, see Chapter 5).

Conclusion

The notion of accreditation of higher education in Latin America is becoming accepted as a systematic, organized and public process. Varying degrees of state dependence are evident, although it is generally considered that accreditation should be handled by the universities themselves, should be voluntary, and should cover both public and private institutions.

Self-evaluation is seen as a useful process, through which the institution monitors overall quality. Its results are valuable for planning and implementing remedial and corrective action, making it a dynamizing element of institutional improvement and growth. Because of its cyclical and participatory nature, it contributes to a greater integration of authorities, administrators, professors and students, underscoring their commitment to the institution and their motivation for creative improvement and renewal. However, Latin American universities generally lack a self-evaluatory culture. Accreditation is perceived to impinge upon institutional autonomy and academic freedom, and many academics still need to be convinced of its positive dimensions.

Nevertheless, there is a widespread conviction regarding the need to promote self-evaluation and accreditation, to ensure that institutions' activities are above the minimum standards of quality and efficiency, and to facilitate a greater exchange between universities within the countries, the regions and the continent as a whole.

Note

All these references, except Sáez, R.S. (1984) relate to papers presented at the International Seminar on University Accreditation in Latin America and the Caribbean, held in Santiago, Chile in December 1991, and organized by CINDA (Centro Interuniversitario de Desarrollo).

References

ALBORNOZ, M.E. (1991) 'Sistema de Evaluación en Universidades: Examinación y Acreditación. La Experiencia Chilena 1981–1991', Universidad de Las Américas, Santiago, Chile.

ALONSO, J.A. (1991) 'La Experiencia de la Pontificia Universidad Católica de Chile como Entidad Examinadora', Universidad Católica de Chile.

ASHTON, A.A. (1991) 'La introducción de un sistema de acreditación en el Caribe de habla inglesa', National Institute of Higher Education, Research Science and Technology, Trinidad, Tobago.

BRUNNER, J.J. (1991) 'Evaluación y Financiamiento de la Educación Superior en América Latina. Bases para un nuevo contrato social', Consejo Superior de Educación, Chile.

CHAPELA, G. (1991) 'Notas sobre el Proceso de creación de un sistema de acreditación de las instituciones de educación superior en México', Universidad Autónoma Metropolitana, México.

COVARRUBIAS, R.G. (1991) 'Visión de la Universidad Mayor sobre el Sistema de Acreditación en Chile', Universidad Mayor, Santiago, Chile.

DE MIGUEL LOPEZ, J.A. (1991) 'La Asociación Dominicana para el Autoestudio y la Acreditación (ADAA). Una Agencia privada de Acreditación Universitaria', ADAA, República Dominicana.

DE REZENDE MARTINS, R.C. (1991) 'El sistema de seguimiento y evaluación de la CAPES: Notas críticas sobre su evaluación', CAPES, Brasil.

GALARZA, J. (1991) 'La Evaluación del Desempeño y la Acreditación Universitaria en Colombia', Universidad del Valle, Cali, Colombia.

LEMAITRE, M.J. (1991) 'El Sistema de Acreditación y el Consejo de Educación Superior', Secretaria Ejecutiva del Consejo Superior de Educación de Chile, Chile.

MARTINEZ, A. (1991) 'La Evaluación Académica e Institucional de la Educación Superior en Colombia', Instituto para el Fomento de la Educación Superior, Colombia.

NEIVA, C.C. (1991) 'La evaluación de la educación superior en Brasil: intentos de formulación de una política en el período 1985–1989', Universidad Federal de Santa Catarina, SC, Brasil.

SÁEZ, R.S. (1984) 'Ciencia Tecnología y Desarrollo' Santiago, SOTEC.

Chapter 3

Asia and the Pacific

Grant Harman

The author attempts an overview of quality issues, traditional methods of quality control, and some new directions in this vast region which includes some of the world's most dynamic economies as well as some of the poorest nations. Developments in China, Hong Kong, India, Korea, Taiwan, The Philippines, New Zealand and Australia are briefly described. The main focus is on universities, as in many cases the information on other post-secondary education sectors is limited.

Introduction

Quality issues dominate the higher education debate in many countries as ministers, bureaucrats, employers and business interests become increasingly concerned about the outputs of tertiary institutions and question whether societies are getting real value for their investment. Central concerns are the maintenance and improvement of levels of teaching and learning, how to define and measure quality, management approaches to improve outcomes, and how to convince or assure major stakeholders that institutions and systems are doing a competent job in ensuring quality outputs.

Various studies have documented key aspects of the debate in OECD countries, and in major geographic regions such as Western Europe and North America (Ball, 1985; National Center for Postsecondary Governance and Finance, 1989; Sizer, 1990; Frazer, 1991; van Vught, 1991; Williams, 1991; Anwyl, 1992; Craft, 1992; Lindsay, 1992; and van Vught and Westerheijden, 1992). Quality is also a major theme in the higher education systems of Asia and the Pacific, although with considerable variation in how the issues are perceived and in government priorities.

Asia and the Pacific is a vast region, containing almost two thirds of the world's population and the world's two largest nations in terms of population — China and India. Geographically it extends from the Indian subcontinent in the west, and sometimes further to include some countries of the Middle East, to Korea and Japan in the north, almost to Hawaii in the east, and including Australia and New Zealand in the south. Its sheer size and diversity of languages, cultures and economic development makes generalization difficult.

In addition, there is very little scholarly literature in English on many of the higher education systems.

Higher Education in the Asia and Pacific Region

With its rapidly growing population and, in many cases, dramatic economic and social changes, the region provides major challenges for higher education providers. It contains some three billion people, many in rural areas. It includes some of the world's fastest growing and dynamic economies, and also some of the poorest nations.

Seven particular points should be noted: First, the higher education systems of the region present a portrait of great diversity. Built on a range of cultural and ideological traditions, they have adapted European and American models to meet local needs. Size varies from relatively small in the Pacific Island states and Papua New Guinea, to the very large systems of India and Japan. Stage of development also varies greatly — some countries enrol less than 1 per cent of the age cohort of 17–24-year-olds, others like Thailand have over 20 per cent participation rate, Japan and Australia even higher. There are differences too in structure, in the roles for the private and public sectors, and in expectations about government financial support and direct control. In the Philippines and Korea, for example, over 80 per cent of enrolments are in private sector institutions, whereas elsewhere the public sector has a virtual monopoly. There is also diversity of resource levels, relations with the labour market, approaches to system-level planning, resource allocation and experimentation. Japan and Australia are well supported compared to Bangladesh, Nepal and some small island nations of the Pacific. In some cases higher and secondary education have expanded at a much faster rate than the economy which has led to rising unemployment among the educated. Many countries are experimenting with open universities, some using the UK Open University model, others introducing different approaches to distance education. Some like Australia and New Zealand are undergoing major reconstruction and reorganization; in others broad policies and overall institutional arrangements have been stable for quite a long period.

Second, higher education in the region has expanded rapidly (see Table 1) and the pressures of growth continue. In Australia and New Zealand, the rate has been modest compared with that in developing countries such as China, the Republic of Korea and Thailand. Australia's 3–5 per cent growth rate per annum since the early 1980s contrasts with the Republic of Korea where enrolments increased from 279,000 in 1977 to 1,364,000 in 1987, with at times an annual growth rate of almost 40 per cent. This places very heavy demands on facilities, staffing and finance; annual fluctuations and significant changes in demand by fields of study place increased strain on institutions.

Third, this expansion has not been matched by an equivalent increase in public funding. Developing countries in particular face major dilemmas: a

Table 1: Expansion of Higher Education in the Asia and Pacific Region

Country	Number of Students per 100,000 inhabitants				
	1975	1980	1985	1986	1987
Australia	2,016	2,203	2,348	2,444	. . .
Bangladesh	207	272	453	445	. . .
Bhutan	. . .	26	17	. . .	. . .
Burma	184	489	. . .	. . .	. . .
China	54	117	168	184	190
Fiji	287	265	335	314	420
Hong Kong	1,012	1,201	1,410	. . .	. . .
India	744	776	. . .	. . .	. . .
Indonesia	205	375	600	. . .	. . .
Japan	2,017	2,065	1,944	1,988	1,971
Korea, Rep. of	903	1,698	3,546	3,634	3,671
Lao People's Dem. Rp	. . .	44	150	. . .	141
Malaysia	. . .	419	604	693	680
Mongolia	683	2,297	. . .	1,984	. . .
Nepal	181	259	414	. . .	. . . .
New Zealand	2,143	2,463	2,950	3,133	3,197
Pakistan	171	182	475	469	. . .
Papua New Guinea	217	163	144	177	. . .
Philippines	1,808	2,641	3,580	. . .	. . .
Singapore	999	963	. . .	. . .	. . .
Sri Lanka	113	288	369	377	. . .
Thailand	317	1,284	1,990	. . .	. . .
Vietnam	167	214	. . .	. . .	. . .

Source: Unesco Statistical Yearbook (revised and reproduced from Meek, 1991, pp. 52–3).

number have invested heavily in higher education over the past three decades, often with support from such agencies as the World Bank and the United Nations Development Programme (UNDP). But now many institutions are confronted with the difficult situation of largely uncontrolled, growth of enrolments and expenditures against a background of diminishing resources, resulting in increased staff–student ratios and staff workloads, and deterioration of working conditions, student services and institutional fabric. Two common coping mechanisms have been the use of open universities with relatively lenient entry requirements and using radio and television to supplement written materials and classroom instruction, and shifting some of the burden to the private sector either through creating private institutions or asking individuals to contribute directly to the cost of their education, or both.

Fourth, the quantitative expansion raises questions concerning the quality of graduates and the nature of graduate competency. Professional skills for ready use in the workplace and specialization for the achievement of specific goals are required by many newly established industries, businesses, and services, whereas flexibility, broad vision, and innovative abilities may be preferred by more established and advanced enterprises. Moral, ethical and personal qualities are also sought. These divergent requirements represent pressure for change and improved efficiency so that institutions may become more closely linked with a nation's economic, social and cultural development.

Fifth, expansion has been accompanied by the growth of new types of institution. Thailand's two open universities cater for almost three-quarters of a million students; China's Radio and Television University System is the largest distance-teaching institution in the world, enrolling 1.61 million students in degree programmes between 1979 and 1989, of whom 1.04 million have graduated and in which since 1986, about three million people have completed subdegree programmes. Private institutions in Indonesia, branches of overseas universities and colleges in Malaysia, regional institutions in Thailand, and the development of polytechnics and training institutes (often in joint schemes with foreign governments or industry) in Singapore, are other strategies to meet demand.

Sixth, despite the diversity, there are some common themes and dilemmas. In addition to those relating to financial support, there are pressures for graduate output to meet labour-market needs, the problem of graduate unemployment, and the difficulty of maintaining and improving quality while at the same time broadening access. In many cases the price of rapid development is high. One Asian observer comments:

> One serious complaint is that the unplanned and haphazard growth of enrolment and the mushrooming of new institutions in many developing countries have alarmingly eroded the quality of the outputs. This relates to both standards and relevance. Unemployment and underemployment of university graduates is widespread. Reports of administrative inefficiency and large-scale waste of resources are not uncommon. Traditional courses of study are still very heavily relied on in many general universities and colleges. Most of them are in the periphery of the international knowledge system and look towards the west for guidance and political change. Their role of teaching, research and public service is indispensable for national development (Selim, undated).

Finally, in most Asian countries demand for student places far exceeds supply. This is not surprising in view of the private benefits higher education is seen to bring and since it is heavily subsidized. Table 2 provides some illustrative data: excess demand varies by field, with medicine and engineering usually the most oversubscribed.

Increasing Concern about Quality

Van Vught and Westerheijden (1992) have drawn attention to four factors to explain the increased attention to quality issues in Western Europe: concern about the level of public expenditure, the expansion of higher education

Table 2: Indicators of Excess Demand for Higher Education in Selected Asian Countries, Mid-1980s

Country	Last graduation in secondary schools	Number taking entry examination	New entrants in higher education institutions		
			local public	local private	distance education
Bangladesh	132580	194764	156389	******	3288
Bhutan	298	..	..	..	..
Burma	133133	..	25151	..	21013
China	2145000	..	809960	0	452344
India	1136075	..	843354	******	4456
Indonesia	519176	983263	97416	142714	40698
Korea	371507	790874	313640	******	39351
Malaysia	146388	..	24499	******	713
Nepal	54611	..	13619	4339	..
Papua New Guinea	828	..	895	******	..
Philippines	660126	595575	64621	321510	..
Sri Lanka	67714	150000	5318	0	3096
Thailand	290409	..	15194	11425	142467

Note: ******: This indicates that student enrolment in local public higher education institutions refers to the new entrants in both public and private local higher education institutions.
Source: Jee-Peng Tan and Alain Mingat (1989) 'Educational Development in Asia: A Comparative Study Focusing on Cost and Financing Issues', World Bank, Asia Technical Department, Report No. ODP 51. (Reproduced from Klitgaard, 1991).

systems, the greater openness in many sectors of present-day societies, and the international mobility of students, teachers and researchers together with the internationalization of the labour market. These all operate in Asia and the Pacific, but in somewhat different form.

Many countries are concerned about the scale of public expenditure and are questioning the priority given to higher education. In Australia and New Zealand, electors have shown a strong desire to reduce taxes and cut public sector budgets, at a time when health costs and social security payments have risen rapidly. In many developing countries education is competing for limited funds with very heavy expenditure needed for essential infrastructure development, especially transport, electricity and irrigation projects. And there is pressure to reduce funds going to higher education so as to expand primary education and give greater priority to adult literacy programs. International agencies have suggested that the rate of return for investment in primary education may be considerably better than for investment in higher education, and this has influenced the policies of aid organizations and sometimes governments. An additional problem for some of the small island nations of the Pacific since the early 1980s has been the major fluctuations in export commodity prices, resulting in fixed or shrinking public sector budgets (Meek, 1992; Gannicott and Throsby, 1990).

As in Europe, rapid expansion in student numbers and in the size and diversity of higher education systems has certainly prompted concern about quality. In Korea and the small South Pacific nations, it is widely believed that expansion has been achieved only at the expense of lowered educational standards. World Bank papers and reports have drawn attention to this problem internationally, noting that:

> the quality of teaching and research has declined as a result of overcrowding, inadequate staffing, deteriorating physical facilities, poor library resources and insufficient scientific equipment. Internal efficiency is often very low and there is a rising problem of mismatch and graduate unemployment. Numerous institutions of higher education in developing countries now operate at the periphery of the international scientific community, unable to engage in the generation and application of the advanced knowledge necessary to address social and economic developed problems (Salmi, 1991, p. 4).

Openness is an important factor in Australia and New Zealand. The climate of accountability demands that government agencies and publicly funded institutions explain to society at large what they are doing and how well they are doing it.

Although operating somewhat differently in this region than in Europe, increasing international mobility of students and the internationalization of the labour market has prompted a new emphasis on academic standards and the standing of degrees. Australia, New Zealand and Japan which are all involved in 'exporting education' are conscious of the need to maintain and enhance quality so as to attract large numbers of fee-paying students. Large numbers of Asian students go abroad to study, and in some countries twinning arrangements are developed with institutions in the US, UK or Australia. Governments are becoming increasingly experienced in making judgments about the quality of academic programs in overseas institutions, whether endorsing international links or in granting academic or professional recognition for overseas qualifications.

An additional factor is economic competition within the region. Governments and industry believe that higher education can play a major role in economic growth and in capitalizing on new opportunities, especially in manufacturing and services. The key attributes are seen to be quality, relevance and flexibility. In Australia, for example, politicians and industrialists stress that quality in higher education will help Australia compete internationally. As a shadow Minister for Education commented:

> Education has to be about excellence . . . If it is not about quality, then all our effort, all our expenditure will have been for nothing because we will not only have blighted the lives of our students, but damaged our ability to compete and survive in a world which does not owe us a living (Kemp, 1992).

The Chief Executive of Australia's largest company was even more explicit:

> We cannot have a world class economy and a world class living standard without a world class workforce. And we cannot have a world class workforce, without world class education (Quoted in Kemp, 1992).

The growth of the private sector of higher education is another factor, sometimes offering high quality and closely monitored education. But in some countries, such as Indonesia, there are concerns that academic standards and teaching are of lower quality than in the public sector.

Finally, as far as developing countries are concerned, some of the new interest in quality stems from changes in the policy of international agencies such as the World Bank, UNDP and UNICEF. During the 1960s and 1970s, their main emphasis was on expansion and growth, with researchers exploring the correlation between earnings and years of schooling. Data to study quality issues was lacking, and influential studies (Coleman, 1966; Jencks, 1972) from the United States seemed to suggest that variations in schooling did not matter much anyway. However, over the past decade, this attitude has been replaced by active interest in quality, which is now explicitly incorporated in the appraisal of education projects, and with some of the data problems overcome (Gannicott and Throsby, 1990).

Quality Issues and Quality Debates

Inadequate resourcing is the single quality issue most frequently identified. For the most part, resourcing per student unit has not kept pace with expansion, and for some less wealthy countries, it is a major problem. In Nepal, for example, it is predicted that over the next three years total student enrolments will double but in real terms public resources for higher education are likely to be reduced by 20 per cent. Even in the developed countries, there is considerable public debate about resource levels. In Australia, despite increases of one-third in real terms since 1983, dollars allocated per equivalent full-time student declined by 11.2 per cent measured against planned load, and by 16.3 per cent measured against actual load (Higher Education Council 1992b, p. 53). What effect this has had on teaching is a matter of dispute.

Academic staffing is a major problem in many developing countries, with an overall shortage of well-qualified staff, serious staff shortages in regional institutions, and unfavourable staff–student ratios. Many systems experience a 'brain drain' from universities to the private sector, where salaries are higher and promotions are on merit, and to overseas appointments.

Students may be inadequately prepared. Secondary education is often weak, especially in mathematics and science, and many students do not have appropriate academic backgrounds to cope with more demanding courses.

In many cases, universities have little influence on the selection, intake, and distribution of students between different courses, which is the responsibility of the government.

Scholars complain of out-of-date curricula and teaching methods, with courses not relevant to development needs. Often there are serious shortages in textbooks and learning materials. And where instruction in English has changed to instruction in the local language, there is often inadequate provision of relevant, up-to-date textbooks.

There is poor internal efficiency: students proceed slowly through the university system, with low progression and graduation rates. There are imbalances in graduate output: systems have often expanded enrolments unnecessarily in the humanities and social sciences at the expense of the sciences and technology. Graduate unemployment remains a major problem, especially on the Indian subcontinent.

In some countries, the supervision of private institutions is minimal and ineffective, and there are now moves to introduce accreditation systems or new registration requirements. For example, in January 1988, the Indonesian Director-General of Higher Education announced a moratorium on the registration of additional private universities, intended to provide breathing space for efforts to improve the quality of those already in existence (Snodgrass, 1991, p. 485). In fact, Indonesia illustrates some of the other issues very vividly. It has a highly centralized major system of public higher education under the control of the Directorate-General of Higher Education (DGHE) and enrolling about 500,000 students, and there is also a private sector with over 750,000 students. Private institutions have more autonomy, but they do come under the control of a Directorate of Private Higher Education in the DGHE. The first major quality problem is the serious shortage of qualified academic staff. In some of the newer universities, and especially those located off Java, this has led to arrangements whereby staff from Jakarta fly in weekly or monthly to take intensive classes. Comparatively few staff even in state universities have higher degrees (Snodgrass, 1991, p. 485–6). Second, there is concern about the standards of teaching. Watson (1992) comments that

university administration is inefficient and the standard of record-keeping low; there are no proper procedures for monitoring course content and teaching; library facilities are inadequate; knowledge of English, the language in which most of the text books are still to be found, is abysmal; the nature of classroom instruction is authoritarian and discourages independent thought. All these factors persist through inertia within the system, largely perpetrated by the staff being appointed from among the graduates of the same institution. Such junior staff tend to follow the practice of mentors and have no other models to adopt. Thus classroom teaching consists almost entirely of a lecturer reading out notes which are duplicated for sale to students. Exams, often multiple choice to avoid the burden of marking, are based simply on these duplicated notes. Not only are students not encouraged to read independently, lecturers themselves rarely read more than a minimum of two or three texts to prepare their courses (Watson, 1992, p. 325).

Third, there is low internal efficiency: many students take seven, eight or more years to complete a course designed to take no more than four to five years and only 10–15 per cent of students complete their courses on time even at leading State universities (Snodgrass, 1991, p. 486). Fourth, the generally low quality of primary and secondary education means that university students are insufficiently prepared for their higher-level studies. Fifth, even though the private institutions do come under government supervision and their graduates have to pass State final examinations to obtain official recognition of their degrees, doubts remain about their quality.

Traditional Methods of Quality Control

Van Vught and Westerheijden (1992) identified two main traditions of quality control in higher education systems in Western Europe (see also Chapter 1). The continental tradition was essentially a tight state-control model, mainly controlling inputs rather than outputs. This included line item budgets, academic staff with civil-servant status, government control over senior academic appointments and staff remuneration, control over student intakes through entrance examinations, control of the approval of new study programs, and sometimes detailed prescription of curriculum and examinations. In some cases a government inspectorate helped monitor quality, while elsewhere there were additional examinations for students to qualify for nationally recognized degrees. By contrast, the British tradition gave individual institutions considerable autonomy through their charters. They were largely left to develop their own forms of quality control, were free to select their own staff according to their own criteria and on their own conditions (including salary levels), to select their own students, to choose their own curriculum, and to award their own degrees. Two key mechanisms for the collective upkeep of academic standards of output were a system of external examiners (experienced academics with a high reputation who reported on student work and examination performance, judging whether it was of comparable quality according to standards applied in other universities) and a system of external accreditation and professional licensing in professional fields such as engineering and accounting.

A third tradition identified in the literature (Her Majesty's Inspectorate, 1991; van Vught, 1991) is the American model. This is based on a reasonably tight budget control for the public sector and some government supervision for private institutions, but allows considerable institutional autonomy for all institutions with respect to curricula, examinations, student admissions and staff appointments. External quality control is exercised mainly through accreditation of institutions and programs carried out by regional agencies, specialist bodies for particular professions, boards which give licences to practice in areas such as accounting and nursing, and state government agencies. The main accreditation agencies are non-government bodies, but operate with a measure of government support. In addition, quality control over admissions is assisted by the national testing organizations. For some observers, the accreditation system seems to

> provide a cost effective assurance that American institutions and programmes meet minimum standards. It also contributes to the improvement of quality in institutions by imposing conditions for accreditation and reaccreditation and through the requirement for self-study which it imposes on institutions. In these ways, accreditation provides an important encouragement to the development of effective quality control by institutions (Her Majesty's Inspectorate, 1991, p. 19).

These three different approaches have each influenced quality in higher education in Asia and the Pacific since the Second World War. In many respects there has been a convergence in the region between the continental bureaucratic and the British models, as many systems based originally on the British-style relatively autonomous universities come under much tighter state control. In most countries the arrangements differ for the separate subsectors (i.e., the universities, polytechnics, teachers' colleges, technical and vocational institutions) with universities generally having much more control over their own affairs, and they also differ for public and private sector.

The Continental or Bureaucratic Model

This model is found in many developing and newly industrialized nations, including Thailand, China, Indonesia, Vietnam and to some extent Korea and Taiwan. Higher education is tightly under government control, with regulations covering the establishment of new institutions, both public and private, and often academic departments, and all aspects of their operation. In many instances, academic staff are civil servants.

In Thailand, for example, the quality of higher education has traditionally been supervised by central-government agencies, especially the Ministry of University Affairs (MUA) which is

> responsible for broad policies relating to higher education, university regulations, setting curriculum standards, overseeing university personnel and administration, for approving accreditation and curriculum development, and for acting as a link between universities and government (Watson, 1991, p. 573).

Through the Joint Higher Education Entrance Examination which it administers, the Ministry controls student selection and admissions, except for the two open universities. For non-university institutions, even tighter control is exercized by other government departments. University curricula and programs are designed within the institution but must be approved by the MUA. College curricula are developed by *ad hoc* committees of representatives from the relevant colleges, and then approved by the Ministry of Education (MOE): According to one Thai scholar, when

> universities and colleges develop a new study program, they require the approval of the curriculum, then apply for permission to operate the program from the MUA and the MOE. Finally they submit the program to the Civil Service Commission to get a salary scale for the graduates of the program (Wiratchai, 1992, p. 725).

The British Model

It is not surprising to find the British model of quality control broadly in use in those nations which were British colonies. In general, universities were given considerable autonomy and were allowed to set their own standards, with external examiners and professional accreditation. Non-government institutions were strictly regulated by government agencies, which frequently set the curricula, recruited the staff and controlled student selection and admission. In many cases legislation required that the academic standard of degrees should be identical to those in British universities. This was the pattern in much of the Indian subcontinent, Malaysia, Brunei, Hong Kong, Singapore, Australia, New Zealand and a number of small Pacific nations. But there are important local variations: for example, there are no external examiners in Australia except for higher research-degree theses.

University autonomy generally has been substantially reduced over recent years. In some cases this has followed from universities' dependence on government funds; elsewhere government control has been used to achieve particular national objectives — for example, affirmative action to achieve ethnic balance in the case of Malaysia (Singh, 1991), and economic competitiveness in Singapore (Selvaratnam, 1992). Many systems following the British model gave considerable responsibility to buffer-type coordinating agencies, along the lines of the former UK University Grants Committee (UGC). But there has been a clear trend away from such bodies, and in many countries, including Australia, New Zealand, Malaysia and Singapore, central ministries of education deal directly with universities and have considerable powers in determining policies. Where the UGC model survives as on the Indian subcontinent, it is more like a government regulatory agency than a committee of academics, and mainly advises government on allocations of funds among institutions. Nevertheless, in India and Pakistan, the UGCs have taken positive measures to try to improve quality by setting up centres or departments of excellence and trying to increase salary levels so as to recruit better qualified staff (Shuka, 1991, Sageb, 1992).

The American Accreditation Model

The Philippines, Korea and Taiwan illustrate features of the American accreditation model. The Philippines has a large higher education system, and both public and private institutions enjoy a large measure of academic autonomy. Some 80 per cent of students are enrolled in private institutions regulated and supervised by the Bureau of Higher Education which formulates minimum standards for their operation and the maintenance of quality education.

This extensive private sector has used American-style voluntary accreditation for some time. It was introduced in Catholic sectarian institutions some thirty years ago, and has now gained wide acceptance among other groups. Accreditation is carried out by separate agencies related to particular associations, such as the Catholic Education Association, the Association of Christian Schools and Colleges, and the Philippine Association of Colleges and Universities, all now joined together in a Federation of Accrediting Agencies of the Philippines (Cooney and Paqueo-Arrezo, 1993). The most advanced is the Philippine Accrediting Association of Schools, Colleges and Universities, established in 1957, and by 1987 accrediting 185 programs in sixty-six different institutions. The government is counterpart Association of State Universities and Colleges which only recently introduced voluntary accreditation.

These agencies' procedures are based on the American pattern of institutional self-examination followed by the visit of a team of peers from other colleges and universities. The visiting committee validates the self-study and then makes recommendations with regard to pre-accreditation, accreditation for three years, and then accreditation for up to seven years. Institutions that achieve high ratings may be exempted from government reinspection and re-evaluation for official recognition, or they may lose recognition if accredited status is not renewed or is withdrawn (Arcelo, 1992). A parallel form of accreditation is operated by professional examination boards in medicine, engineering, nursing, law and accounting. And the Department of Education, Culture and Sports maintains technical panels in seven major disciplinary areas which have the power to recommend opening or phasing out curricula in non-government institutions.

A second external quality control mechanism consists of testing bodies, which examine students wishing to enter higher education. A National College Entrance Examination is operated by the National Education Testing and Research Centre. Other national examinations for university entry to particular university professional schools are conducted by the Centre for Education Measurement, a private testing agency 'whose mission is to enhance excellence in education through test and measurement' (Arcelo, 1992) and other bodies.

The limitations of these three traditional methods of quality control in the region need to be stressed. In many cases, the emphasis has been mainly on control of inputs, with comparatively little attention given at system level to assessment of educational processes and outputs. Moreover, at institutional level, there has been little capacity to monitor educational performance in any systematic manner. Many developing and newly industrialized countries lack a strong tradition of evaluation in higher education, even though the need for improvement and better use of resources is pressing (Teichler and Winkler, 1991).

Further, as already noted, the existing methods of quality control in many countries of the region are based on highly regulated State control and intervention. A number of scholars have speculated that this may be one reason why many of these systems are so sluggish in their response to calls for change and innovation. A leading Indian economist, Patel, is even more critical. In an address to a 1991 World Bank seminar in Kuala Lumpur, he said:

it has to be admitted that despite much governmental interference in everything, including appointments and promotions — and perhaps because of it — the system of efficiency and performance audit in higher education leaves much to be desired in most developing countries. This is undoubtedly one of the main causes of high costs and poor quality . . . Restoring a semblance of management and managerial autonomy by rolling back government intervention and political patronage and making students and teachers responsive to purely educational criteria are perhaps the greatest challenges in higher education in many developing societies (Patel, 1991, p. 12).

New Directions

Some Asia and Pacific countries are currently experimenting with new forms of quality control and quality assurance, or are considering doing so. In most cases, the initiative has come from governments and government agencies; elsewhere, the institutions themselves have played an important role. Some examples from China, Hong Kong, Korea, Taiwan, the Philippines, New Zealand and Australia are briefly described below. Although these reflect a range of models and mechanisms, common features are a concern with educational processes and outcomes, and the inclusion of self-studies and or detailed documentation, with visits to institutions by panels of experts. Because of the author's easier access to information, the New Zealand and Australian experience is dealt with in greater detail.

China

China is attempting to introduce national evaluation mechanisms. One major effort concentrating on academic disciplines was introduced in 1985, and by 1993 eight disciplines encompassing fifty-five degrees had been reviewed (Sensicle, 1993). Another major effort has been the review of masters and doctoral degrees, with appraisal groups and peer experts, appointed by the Academic Degrees Committee of the State Council. By 1992, more than 100 doctoral and 1,000 masters programs had been reviewed in the humanities and social sciences, natural sciences, engineering, agriculture and medicine (Wang and Li, 1993) using criteria and procedures set by the Academic Degrees Committee. Major emphasis is placed on self-study by academic units, which submit detailed reports to the Committee. Shortage of funds and differences between institutions has made it difficult to continue these nationwide reviews, and the Committee is gradually delegating masters' degree evaluation to relevant ministries and provinces.

Hong Kong

In 1990 the Hong Kong government established the Hong Kong Council for Academic Accreditation. Modelled on the British Council for National Academic Awards, this body monitors academic standards, accredits institutions and validates degree courses in the non-university sector (Tsim, 1992, Sensicle, 1992). The accreditation process commences with a detailed proposal submitted by an institution. A panel of four or five experts is appointed, visits the institution and then reports to the Council. A notable feature is that each panel includes several experts from outside Hong Kong (usually from the UK, the US and/or Australia). The Hong Kong universities lobbied hard to ensure that they were not subject to validation and review by the Council, arguing that their own internal procedures are rigorous and are supplemented by professional body accreditation and with one exception, by the external examiner system.

India

The University Grants Commission has statutory responsibilities to determine and maintain standards of teaching, examinations and research in universities. Its recent initiatives include setting up academic staff colleges to provide in-service and refresher courses for university teachers; a scheme of restructuring undergraduate programs to achieve increased flexibility and greater social relevance; establishment of inter-university audio-visual and educational media research centres, and a 'National Educational Testing Programme'. It has also explored the possibility of developing a system of accreditation for higher education institutions (Khanna and Sharma, 1993).

The work of specialist agencies has been particularly important in the case of medicine and technical education. The Medical Council of India, established by an Act of Parliament consists of medical educators, practising experts, and appointees from ministries of health at state and national levels. It prescribes minimum standards for medical courses and facilities, carries out inspections, and has the power to withdraw accreditation from institutions whereupon their medical graduates may not be registered as practitioners (Shuka, 1991).

Similar supervision of engineering and technical education is provided by the All India Council of Technical Education, set up under the authority of the Ministry of Education. This functions through specialist Boards of Studies for particular disciplines. New course proposals in technical education are sent to the relevant professional body; experts evaluate them and examine the infrastructure and facilities, and on their recommendation the Council may grant or withhold approval (Behar, 1992). The Bar Council of India, the Indian Council of Medical Research, the Institute of Chartered Accountants and the Institution of Engineers are also active, and most maintain close links with parallel bodies in the UK and elsewhere.

Korea

Leaders of higher education institutions in Korea generally believe that over the past two decades or so the government allowed far too rapid expansion at the expense of quality. At a recent World Bank senior policy seminar, the President of the University of Ulsam commented that

> the rapid expansion of, and equalization in, higher education, has posed a quality problem. The quantitative expansion naturally resulted in recruiting mediocre high school graduates in universities . . .

> The abrupt increase in student population has given rise to serious deficiencies in facilities and professors . . . the Korean university is deeply entangled with the conflicting dilemma of quantity versus quality (Lee, 1992).

At the same seminar, the President of Pohang Institute of Science and Technology said that through quantitative expansion 'quality had inevitably suffered' and that university

> education in science and engineering which had begun without any research projects still has no research activities in many colleges and universities today. With an exception of two or three universities, the masters and doctoral degrees conferred in science and engineering at Korean Universities are questionable in their academic standard (Kim, 1992, p. 14).

Two important recent developments have sprung from this concern. First, tight Ministry of Education control has been somewhat relaxed and the government is encouraging institutions towards more autonomous academic planning and development in combination with increased financial support. Universities are now largely responsible for senior appointments, curriculum planning and development, and student discipline, and government financial support is being provided for academic research and for overseas study grants. Policy has changed from 'control without sufficient support' to 'more support without strong control' (Lee, 1993).

Second, a comprehensive system of university accreditation is being introduced, following earlier activities of the Korean Council for University Education which since 1984 has undertaken institutional evaluations in five-year cycles, and program evaluations on an annual basis. Program accreditation began in 1991, although institutional accreditation is being delayed until 1996. Departments in two selected fields are assessed each year. Self evaluations by each department are followed by on-site visits of specialist panels. The results are analysed by the Korean Council for University Education and a list of universities with 'sound' departments is published (see also Chapter 7).

Taiwan

Since 1991 efforts have been under way to improve the system of specialized accreditation of programs and institutions operated for some years by the Ministry of Education. Opinions were collected from educators and institutional administrators through an extensive series of seminars, leading to the suggestion that specialized accreditation should be carried out by academic associations, rather than the Ministry. As a result, the Ministry funded a feasibility study and trial whereby three associations are formulating implementation plans, holding seminars for evaluators, conducting self-studies and on-site evaluations, and publishing evaluation reports. The trial will be completed during 1994, and it is widely expected that responsibility for all specialized accreditation will be handed over to the academic associations. Possibly the Ministry will play a somewhat similar role to the Council on Postsecondary Accreditation in the United States, accrediting the associations that will in turn carry out the specialized accreditation (Su, 1993).

The Philippines

As already noted, an American-style system of voluntary accreditation was developed more than three decades ago in the Philippines private sector, and has more recently been extended to state universities and colleges.

Accreditation status is categorized into four levels:

- Level 1 — institutions that are undertaking the accreditation process;
- Level 2 — accredited institutions;
- Level 3 — institutions with accredited status that have achieved significant academic research and extension services; and
- Level 4 — institutions considered to be national centres of excellence.

Level 1 institutions get some financial support for undertaking accreditation efforts. Level 2 institutions are entitled to financial deregulation and academic autonomy. Level 3 institutions gain greater recognition with greater financial support as they move towards being considered national centres of excellence. No institution has yet been categorized as Level 4 (Arcelo, 1992, pp. 13–14).

The Federation of Accrediting Agencies of the Philippines has developed common accrediting standards, and in 1991 the Congressional Commission on Education recommended that the policies and practices of the accrediting agencies be reviewed periodically (Cooney and Paqueo-Arrezo, 1993).

New Zealand

As part of major reforms to its education system, the New Zealand government recently established new mechanisms of quality control, quality assurance and quality improvement for post-school education. These mechanisms are operated by the New Zealand Qualifications Authority (NZQA), (described fully in Chapter 8), the New Zealand Vice-Chancellors Committee (NZVCC), the Education Review Office, and the Ministry of Education, and apply to both universities and non-university institutions. The changes were preceded by extensive community consultations and intensive investigations of the tertiary education and training system, and culminated in the 1990 Education Amendment Act, which listed as one of its major aims the intention to give tertiary institutions 'as much independence and freedom to make academic, operational and management decisions as is consistent with the nature of the services they provide, the efficient use of national resources, the national interest and the demands of accountability' (Langer, 1991).

The NZQA is responsible for approval of all nationally recognized tertiary education programs, except for those in universities which have been delegated to the NZVCC. The NZVCC has been more formally established and has inherited key functions of the former University Grants Committee, a buffer body between universities and the Ministry. The NZVCC now approves all new degree courses, moderates standards, and administers scholarships for universities. For all other tertiary institutions, the NZQA accredits courses, accredits them to teach nationally recognized courses including degrees, and monitors educational standards. Its governing body of leading businessmen, industrialists and representatives from school and tertiary education is appointed by the Ministry. In due course it is intended to become fully self-funding.

A major task for the NZQA has been to establish a qualifications' framework, and a database of all registered units, courses, and tertiary education providers. Theoretically any registered provider can teach any registered course. The essential thrust for its establishment came from concerns about vocational education, and the desire to develop a competency-based approach to training and facilitate credit transfer. The qualifications system it has developed was derived, to some extent, from the work of the Scottish Vocational Council, and the National Council for Vocational Qualifications in the United Kingdom. It is mandated to assess the quality of tertiary education and to assure itself that quality control and quality assurance systems are in place in institutions, and in the long-term its main function will be quality audit. Quality is not specifically defined but elements mentioned are conforming to specifications, fitness for purpose, and responsiveness, viz:

> There are many definitions of quality but there is general agreement that quality is present when specified requirements are met . . . If quality is the meeting of requirements, then quality can only be measured if these requirements are known and defined. By defining requirements, the standards to be achieved are set (New Zealand Qualifications Authority, 1992, p. 7).

On this basis, the NZQA has concentrated on developing indicators of quality and helping institutions to develop their own quality measures. Its twin thrusts are validation and moderation. Validation criteria include such checklist items as the following:

- the course is described in terms of learning objectives;
- the course provides a sound and balanced learning progression;
- assessment procedures are well-documented, educationally sound, relate to the course objectives, and are understood by the learner;
- prerequisites and admission requirements are appropriate and fair;
- the administrative, financial and professional provision are adequate to support the course;
- accommodation and learning facilities are relevant, current, adequate and accessible; and
- student facilities and support services meet acceptable standards and cultural and equity requirements (Cliff, 1992).

Although documentation details how validation will be conducted, it does not specify the basis for evaluation, and this has provided some problems for visiting validation teams. So far there has been little input from students in these procedures, except for a brief meeting between the validation team and selected students. On moderation, the NZQA stresses the need for self-evaluation in conjunction with peer evaluation.

Although the universities have not been directly affected by the work of the NZQA, some observers believe that in time some universities may wish to be recognized as national providers and to have courses and units recognized nationally. Apart from this, the work of the Authority has prompted the universities to look more closely at their internal academic accreditation processes and to establish an academic audit unit for the university system (Malcolm, 1993).

Both the NZQA and the Education Review Office were intended to have rights of entry to institutions, but this provision was removed from the original bill following strong national and international opposition to what was perceived to be a serious threat to academic freedom. The Education Review Office's functions are now limited to a three-yearly review of the extent to which higher education institutions are eliminating barriers to disadvantaged groups and actively promoting equity. Through these two agencies, the government has considerable power to determine directions for higher education and monitor performance, although the powers are somewhat less easily exercized for universities (Peddie, 1992, p. 507).

As the major funding provider, the Ministry of Education is concerned primarily with resource allocation and utilization, but it does have a substantial interest in educational quality, and can direct an institution not to provide a course of study (but not an individual section of a course) where resources could be used inefficiently. Polytechnics are required to report on performance and the Ministry employs various performance indicators including costs per student, staff–student ratio, and operating surplus or deficit. It requires each polytechnic to report on achievements in relation to goals and objectives as stated in its business plan, but the measures used tend to be descriptive rather than quantitative and provide a fairly restricted set of quality measures. Polytechnics:

> do not have a formal means of establishing whether their individual performance met, exceeded or fell short of the Ministry's expectations. It appears the polytechnics will have to rely on their own comparison methods and other informal ways to determine the Ministry's level of satisfaction with their performance (Cliff, 1992).

Australia

The University and Technical and Further Education (TAFE) systems in Australia have both experimented with a number of new quality control, quality assurance and quality improvement mechanisms over recent years. The main driving force has been the Commonwealth or Federal government; although most institutions are owned and operated by state governments, the Commonwealth government essentially provides the basic operating grants of all universities and a substantial proportion of funds for TAFE colleges.

The universities have largely used a traditional British-style approach to quality control, with strict regulations for student admissions, course approval checks at department, faculty and academic board levels, periodic reviews of courses and departments and efforts to improve teaching through the work of special teaching and learning centres, (although few use external examiners at undergraduate level). At system level, the main mechanisms were periodic reviews by major Commonwealth and state government committees of enquiry, and accreditation by professional associations and, in a limited number of cases, by state registration boards for professions.

By the mid 1980s it was clear that this approach was unsatisfactory. A major study of quality measures for universities, concluded that:

> with the exception of certain areas, Australian universities have yet to perfect in their own walls that culture of evaluation and self-assessment, especially at the department level, which is an integral part of any professional activity (Bourke, 1986, p. 20).

About the same time, the Commonwealth Tertiary Education Commission decided that higher education institutions needed to develop procedures for systematic evaluation 'which will enable them to demonstrate that they are seeking at all times to preserve and enhance the quality of their activities (Commonwealth Tertiary Education Commission 1986, p. 262). Commonwealth ministers responsible for higher education began to emphasize the need for a more serious approach to evaluation, and in 1991, stated that there was concern that in the recent rapid expansion 'quality had been sacrificed to numbers' and that the government considered it necessary to 'implement measures specifically designed to provide a degree of quality assurance at both institutional level and for the higher education system as a whole' (Baldwin, 1991, p. 3). Federal measures instituted since the mid-1980s include:

- a system of discipline reviews carried out by panels of experts which report to the Minister;
- a project to develop and test performance indicators which might be useful in the evaluation of university activities;
- allocation of funds from the National Priority (Reserve) Fund to support curriculum development or projects to improve quality;
- establishment of a fund for institutional projects to improve teaching, administered by the Committee for the Advancement of University Teaching; and
- establishment of a national academic audit mechanism to review the procedures used by universities for monitoring and improving the quality of outcomes.

In addition, in 1987 the Australian Vice-Chancellors' Committee introduced academic standards panels.

Of these various initiatives, the discipline reviews, the academic standards' panels and the new audit mechanism deserve special comment. The discipline reviews, established by the then Commonwealth Tertiary Education Commission in 1985, have focused on major disciplines and fields of professional education (law, engineering, teacher education in mathematics and science, accounting, agriculture, information science). Their terms of reference have required expert panels to consider qualitative aspects of teaching and learning, and also to investigate supply and demand for graduates, questions of duplication and rationalization of offerings, and resource utilization. Their original aim was to:

> determine whether the teaching and research activities of higher education institutions in particular fields of study were carried out at a suitable level, whether there were any areas where resources were wasted or where there was duplication and whether there were ways in which quality and efficiency might be improved (Chubb, 1991).

Panel members have been drawn from senior academics, the professions and major employers of graduates. While the various reviews completed have been competent pieces of policy research, Connell claims that the first four reviews failed to assess teaching and learning (Connell, 1992, pp. 40–1). Further, there is debate about the extent to which the reviews have operated as a stimulus for change and self-appraisal, and it is generally agreed that the process has proved slow-moving and expensive. The current government plan is to continue the reviews, 'but on a less costly and probably more frequent basis' (Higher Education Council, 1992b, p. 76).

Academic standards' panels were established in 1987 by the Australian Vice-Chancellors Committee rather than the government. Made up of five to seven experts drawn from Australian universities, the panels have been concerned mainly with consistency of grading in fourth-year honours courses in a number of basic disciplines (Lee Dow, 1992). The Vice-Chancellors' Committee considered using external examiners, but chose the panels because of lesser costs involved and the possibility of producing greater interaction between senior university personnel in particular disciplines.

The recently established national academic audit mechanism has some novel features. Following eighteen months of extensive consultation with the universities and relevant interest groups by the Higher Education Council, the Commonwealth government's main advisory body for higher education policy, the Minister for Higher Education and Employment Services announced:

> The Government's principal initiative in relation to quality is its decision to provide additional funds of $70 million, the equivalent of 2 per cent of operating grants, annually from 1994 for a quality assurance and enhancement program. These funds, which are additional to the operating grants provided for 1994, are intended to act as a catalyst

for institutions to allocate their total resources in ways which will maximize the quality of provision. The funds will be allocated in recognition of good performance in the use of all available resources to attain the best quality, including the achievement of equity objectives, taking into account such factors as quality management practices, the composition of the student population and the extent of progress in implementing articulation and credit transfer arrangements (Baldwin, 1991, pp. 33–4).

As a result of its consultations, the Higher Education Council was able to recommend a mechanism which appeared to have a much wider degree of university support than many people had thought possible. Its formal report to the Minister, *Achieving Quality*, argued that while discipline reviews and academic standards' panels are useful 'they are not sufficiently systematic, comprehensive in their coverage, not representative enough of all stakeholders, to provide quality assurance for the system as a whole' (Higher Education Council, 1992a, p. 76).

After considering a range of possible structures for a quality assurance agency from an inspectorate through to a two-level agency with separate audit and quality improvement functions, the Council recommended a separate committee, responsible to the Minister through the Higher Education Council and composed of experts drawn from both higher education and the wider community. It recommended that the committee should:

- invite universities to participate in regular review and audit of their mechanisms for monitoring and improving quality of their outcomes;
- examine portfolios submitted by universities showing the quality assurance and quality improvement mechanisms in place;
- conduct interviews and visits and evaluate how institutions have assessed the effects of their policies and processes; and
- recommend to the Minister on the allocation of specially designated funds to universities to recognize achievements demonstrated by the effectiveness of policies and procedures through an evaluation of their assessment of the quality of their outcomes.

The essential idea is to have a quality assurance mechanism somewhat wider in its scope than that of the former UK Academic Audit Unit, yet sensitive to university claims about the importance of institutional autonomy and Australian dislike of élite-type ranking systems. The limited measure of performance funding involves additional funds, and there is no intention to use the committee's recommendations to allocate general operating grants to institutions. The funding element is intended as an incentive to secure participation by universities in the scheme, and to recognize and reward institutions which have in place quality mechanisms which are demonstrably effective. The main emphasis is not to monitor performance, but to evaluate what universities actually do and achieve in quality control; in other words, the emphasis is on quality management and quality achievement and ranking will be on this basis and 'not because of what universities are or do, or because of how old (or young) they are'.

Each year, the committee is to select a particular area of work to be audited, and invite universities to submit a portfolio of documentation, setting out both policies and processes in place, and their own assessment of outcomes in relation to institutional missions and objectives. Key aspects of university activities are to be covered over a period of three to five years.

A Committee for Quality Assurance in Higher Education was appointed with a senior Vice-Chancellor as Chair, and in July 1993 guidelines were issued and universities were invited to participate. The guidelines departed somewhat from the original plan by stating that the reviews would focus on quality outcomes as well as on quality assurance processes. In 1993, the Committee undertook an overview study of institutional quality assurance policies and practices; for 1994 the emphasis is on teaching and learning, with the management and integration of research and community service activities most likely to follow. Funding criteria set by the Minister specify that only about half the universities will gain a share of the additional funds, and that the maximum to be awarded to any university will be an amount equal to 5 per cent of its operating budget.

In the TAFE sector, a rapid increase in the number of non-government providers and other concerns about quality have prompted the development of new accreditation and regulatory agencies at state and territory level, independent from major government providers. Previously TAFE courses were internally accredited by the major providers, with accredited awards being simply registered nationally with a joint Commonwealth-state agency.

Another development is the introduction of a national competency-based approach to vocational education with definition and listing of employment-related key competencies, national curriculum principles, and an Australian Vocational Certificate Training System. While this does not essentially spring from a quality control or quality assurance agenda, it has the potential to have a major impact on evaluation and assessment in TAFE colleges, whose work is likely to be subject to a much greater degree of external assessment. Significantly the idea of competency-based training and the wider national reform agenda is being supported by Commonwealth and state governments as well as by professional associations, employer groups and the trade unions, with the latter group taking an active interest in the definition and assessment of competencies.

Conclusion

Quality is a major issue in higher education in Asia and the Pacific, although within the region there are very considerable variations about how quality issues are perceived and in the priorities of governments and institutions. Concern about quality of educational programmes is clearly increasing, reflecting the rapid expansion in student enrolments, the growth of the private sector, and increasing pressures arising from international economic competition. In the region, discussion of quality issues focuses not only on quality assurance, but on inadequacies with respect to resources, staff, facilities and curricula, and on problems such as imbalances in graduate output and graduate unemployment.

There are experiments with new forms of quality assurance, particularly academic accreditation, academic audit, performance funding, discipline reviews, and new qualifications frameworks and competency-based approaches to vocational training. Many seem likely to continue and expand in scope, especially if they are able to produce positive benefits such as improvements in academic programmes, closer links with employers and professions, and increased portability of professional qualifications. On the other hand, questions are already being asked about the financial and administrative costs in relation to the benefits derived, while in the poorest countries inadequacy of resources seems likely to continue well into the future as the single most pressing quality problem.

References

ANWYL, J. (1992) *Quality in Higher Education: Proceedings of the National Invitational Workshop held at the University of Melbourne*, Centre for the Study of Higher Education, University of Melbourne, Parkville.

ARCELO, A. (1992) 'Governance and Management Issues in Philippine Higher Education', Paper presented at World Bank Seminar, Singapore.

BALL, C. (1985) *Fitness for Purpose*, SRHE and NFER-Nelson, Guildford.

BEHAR, S.C. (1992) 'India', in CLARK, B.R. and NEAVE, G. (Eds) *Encyclopedia of Higher Education*, Pergamon Press, Oxford.

BOURKE, P. (1986) *Quality Measures in Universities*, Commonwealth Tertiary Education Commission, Canberra.

CHUBB, I. (1991) The Higher Education Council, Address to Heads and Deans Seminar at the University of Melbourne, Parkville.

CLIFF, A. (1992) Measuring Quality in New Zealand Polytechnics, Paper presented at Australasian Institute of Tertiary Education Administrators Conference, Ballarat.

COLEMAN, J.S. (1966) *Equality of Educational Opportunity*, US Government Printing Office, Washington.

COMMONWEALTH TERTIARY EDUCATION COMMISSION (1986) *Review of Efficiency and Effectiveness in Higher Education*, Australian Government Publishing Service, Canberra.

CONNELL, W.F. (1992) 'Reviewing the quality of higher education', *The Australian Universities Review*, 35, pp. 36–41.

COONEY, R.P. and PAQUEO-ARREZO, E. (1993) 'Higher education regulation in the Philippines: Issues of control, quality assurance and accreditation', *Higher Education Policy*, 6, 2, pp. 25–8.

CRAFT, A. (Ed) (1992) *Quality Assurance in Higher Education*, London, Falmer Press.

FRAZER, M. (1991) 'Quality Assurance in Higher Education', Council for National Academic Awards, London.

GANNICOTT, H.K. and THROSBY, C.D. (1990) 'The Quality of Education in the South Pacific: Some Preliminary Hypotheses', unpublished paper, Canberra.

HER MAJESTY'S INSPECTORATE (1991) *Education Observed: Aspects of Education in the USA — Quality and its Assurance in Higher Education*, HMSO, London.

BALDWIN, P. (1991) *Higher Education: Quality and Diversity in the 1990's*, Policy Statement by the Hon, Peter Baldwin, MP, Minister for Higher Education and Employment Services, Australian Government Publishing Service, Canberra.

HIGHER EDUCATION COUNCIL (1992a) *Achieving Quality*, Australian Government Publishing Service, Canberra.

HIGHER EDUCATION COUNCIL (1992b) *The Quality of Higher Education: Discussion Papers*, Australian Government Publishing Service, Canberra.

JENCKS, C. (1972) *Inequality: A Reassessment of the Effect of Family and Schooling in America*, Basic Books, New York.

KEMP, D. (1992) 'National press club address', Canberra, July.

KHANNA, S.K. and SHARMA, G.D. (1993) 'Measures of Quality Assurance in Higher Education: An Indian Experience', Paper presented at the INQAAHE conference, Montreal, Canada.

KIM, R. (1991) 'Republic of Korea', in ALTBACH, P.G. (Ed) *International Higher Education: An Encyclopedia*, Garland Publishing, New York.

KIM, H. (1992) 'The contribution of public and private education to development in Asian higher education', Paper presented at World Bank Seminar, Singapore.

LANGER, R.H.M. (1991) 'The universities of New Zealand', in *Commonwealth Universities Yearbook*, Association of Commonwealth Universities, London.

LEE, SANG-JOU (1992) 'Higher Education in Korea: Current Trends and Problems', Paper presented at World Bank Senior Policy Seminar, Singapore, 28 June–2 July.

LEE, WHA-KUK (1993) 'Issues in the Development of University Accreditation in Korea', Paper presented at the INQAAHE conference, Montreal, Canada.

LEE DOW, K. (1992) 'Academic Standards Panels in Australia', in CRAFT, A. (Ed) op. cit.

LINDSAY, A.W. (1992) 'Concepts of Quality in Higher Education', *Journal of Tertiary Education Administration*, 14, 2, pp. 153–63.

MALCOLM, W. (1993) 'The Development of an Academic Audit Unit in New Zealand', paper presented at INQAAHE conference, Montreal, Canada.

MEEK, V.L. (1992) 'Quality and Relevance of Higher Education in Small States', Paper prepared for World Bank Seminar, Brunei.

NATIONAL CENTER FOR POSTSECONDARY GOVERNANCE AND FINANCE (1989) *Quality in the Academy: Proceedings from a National Symposium*, University of Maryland, College Park.

NEAVE, M. (1991) *Models of Quality Assurance in Europe*, CNAA, London.

NEW ZEALAND QUALIFICATIONS AUTHORITY (1992) *Quality Management Systems for Nationally Registered Qualifications: A Draft Discussion Document*, NZQA, Wellington.

PATEL, I.G. (1991) 'Higher Education and Economic Development: Keynote Address', World Bank Seminar, Kuala Lumpur.

PEDDIE, R. (1992) 'New Zealand', in CLARK, B.R. and NEAVE, G. (Eds), *Encyclopedia of Higher Education*, Pergamon Press, Oxford.

SALMI, J. (1991) *Perceptions on the Financing of Higher Education*, Education and Employment Division, The World Bank, Washington.

SAGEB, G.N. (1992) 'Pakistan', in CLARK, B.R. and NEAVE, G. (Ed) *Encyclopedia of Higher Education*, Pergamon Press, Oxford.

SELIM, M. (undated) 'Higher Education in Asia and the Pacific', Bangkok.

SELVARATNAM, V. (1992) 'Innovations in Higher Education: Singapore at the Competitive Edge', Education and Employment Division, The World Bank, Washington.

SENSICLE, A. (1992) 'The Hong Kong Initiative', in CRAFT, A. (Ed) *Quality Assurance in Higher Education*, London, Falmer Press.

SENSICLE, A. (1993) 'One Country, Two (Education) Systems: Hong Kong', Paper presented at the INQAAHE conference, Montreal, Canada.

SHUKA, S. (1991) 'India', in ALTBACH, P.G. (Ed) *Higher Education: An Encyclopedia*, Garland Publishing, New York.

SINGH, J.S. (1991) 'Malaysia', in ALTBACH, P.G. (Ed) *International Higher Education: An Encyclopedia*, Garland Publishing, New York.

SIZER, J. (1990) 'Funding councils and performance indicators in quality assessment in the United Kingdom', in GOEDEGEBURRE, L.C.J., MAASSEN, P.A.M. and WESTENHEIJDEN, D.F. (Eds) *Peer Review and Performance Indicators*, Lemme, Utrecht.

SNODGRASS, D.R. (1991) 'Indonesia', in ALTBACH, P.G. (Ed) *International Higher Education: An Encyclopedia*, Garland Publishing, New York.

SU, JIN-LI (1993) Specialized Accreditation in Taiwan: Issues and Perspectives, Paper presented at the INQAAHE conference Montreal, Canada.

TEICHLER, U. and WINKLER, H. (1991) 'Performance of Higher Education: Measurement for Improvement-Evaluation of Outcomes', Paper presented to World Bank Higher Education Seminar, Kuala Lumpur.

TSIM, T.L. (1992) 'The Universities of Hong Kong', in *Commonwealth Universities Yearbook 1992*, The Association of Commonwealth Universities, London.

VUGHT, VAN F.A. (1991) 'Higher Education Quality Assessment in Europe: the next step', Keynote address of 39th bi-annual conference of the Standing Conference of Rectors, Presidents and Vice-Chancellors of the European Universities, Utrecht, The Netherlands, 17–18 October.

VUGHT, VAN F.A. and WESTERHEIJDEN, D.F. (1992) *Quality Management and Quality Assurance in European Higher Education: Methods and Mechanisms*, Center for Higher Education Policy Studies, University of Twente, Enschede.

WANG, Z. and LI, J. (1993) 'Academic Degrees Accreditation and Evaluation in China', Paper presented at the INQAAHE conference, Montreal, Canada.

WIRATCHAI, N. (1992) 'Thailand', in CLARK, B.R. and NEAVE, G. (Eds) *The Encylopedia of Higher Education*, Pergamon Press, Oxford.

WATSON, C.W. (1992) 'Indonesia', in CLARK, B.R. and NEAVE, G. (Eds) *The Encyclopedia of Higher Education*, Pergamon Press, Oxford.

WILLIAMS, P.R. (1991) *The CVCP Academic Audit Unit*, Birmingham.

Chapter 4

Africa

Juma Shabani

Quality in African higher education has suffered seriously as it struggles with massive expansion in a context of profound political, social and economic changes and severe financial crisis. The author indicates some current strategies in response, which include the regionalization of training institutions and the development of institutional networks, and outlines the contribution of the Association of African Universities.[1]

The Current Situation

During the past decade the environment in which African universities have operated has undergone many profound political, social and economic changes, compelling the universities to revise radically not only their objectives but also their mission, strategies, structures and even their modes of operation. Of the crises confronting the higher education system, those caused by finance and growth have been the greatest cause of deteriorating quality.

Financial Crisis

For years the African university has had to face an acute financial crisis characterized by considerable reduction both in state subsidies and in financial support from the international community. Budget allocations by government to the universities, which make up 90 per cent of their funds, have been reduced constantly, in the context of a dire economic situation caused by the increase in debt servicing, the fall in the prices of raw materials and agricultural products, the devaluation of national currencies, the implementation of structural adjustment policies and so on. At the same time, a large portion of the funds formerly given to higher education in Africa by the international community has in recent years been reallocated to basic education.

This reduction in funds has made it impossible for African universities to procure the basic equipment, books and scientific journals indispensable for teaching and research. As a result, some universities are compelled to cancel practical work or reduce it to a minimum, which is highly detrimental. Practical work helps to improve the quality of training, leading the student to a better understanding of the content and implications of certain theoretical concepts, especially where the teaching syllabus, if there is any, may constitute the documentation available.

Nor are the lecturers certain of finding the necessary documentation enabling them to update teaching content and methods, in order to train students capable of responding to social changes and the rapid development of knowledge and skills. In some countries, the financial crisis is so acute that the universities cannot even pay the salaries of lecturers. Three tendencies can be observed:

- Lecturers leave the country to work in universities offering better working conditions thereby increasing the incidence of brain drain.
- Lecturers leave the university to work in private enterprises within the country. That constitutes brain recycling.
- Lecturers remain on campus but spend most of their time trading or in other income-generating activities. Such lecturers make no effort to improve the quality of their teaching or to update their knowledge. This has been called brain-leakage.

These phenomena deprive African universities of a good number of their highly qualified staff capable of playing a decisive role in the promotion and improvement of the quality of teaching.

To the groups mentioned should be added an increasing number of lecturers who devote most of their time to political activities, particularly within the framework of political parties and trade union movements, while remaining on campus.

The Crisis of Growth

African universities have experienced extremely rapid growth in student numbers, and especially first-year students. Unfortunately, this has not been accompanied by a commensurate development of infrastructure, human and material resources. As an example, the University of Yaoundé, Cameroon which opened in 1960 with 500 students, by 1992 had 45,000 students with facilities planned for 5,000.

During the 1990–1 academic year, the students registered for the first year in all four faculties of the University of Dakar made up 68.32 per cent of the 22,000 students of the university. In the Faculty of Law and Economics, first-year students made up 80 per cent of enrolments.

It is quite obvious that such an expansion should have taken into account adequate extension of facilities and equipment to meet the needs of scientific training and ensure appropriate teaching methods. It calls especially for development in the number and quality of teaching staff, in order to maintain the requisite standards.

Regrettably, however, African countries did not adopt clear and coherent policies of university development, especially in the area of infrastructural and human-resource development in equal step with the growth in student numbers. Thus it is not unusual for instance, to see a lecture hall designed for 800 students packed with as many as 3,000. Hardly a good framework for teaching, having more in common with markets and stadia than with places for reflection. In such a situation, access to knowledge is, largely, determined by the ability to arrive four or five hours in advance to occupy the best place to hear the lecturer.

The ratio of one lecturer to 150 students in some universities compares very badly to that in industrialized countries. And in terms of quality, the teaching-staff pyramid is very flat with regard to the initial grades of teaching assistants and senior teaching assistants, and sharply pointed with regard to professors.

In the higher classes, student numbers are not so great and teaching is done under better conditions. However, the lack of teaching materials and the inadequate practical training of the earlier classes show their effects in the form of serious gaps in knowledge. The inevitable need to conduct remedial classes results in delays in carrying through teaching programmes some aspects of which are taught superficially just to complete the work on the academic schedule.

The deterioration of quality is aggravated by the fact that the few lecturers available have to do everything, from conducting the main course to the supervision of end-of-course work, class exercises, provision of services to the community, working on various national technical commissions and so on.

The problem of managing the increase in student populations is not easy to solve, especially since in some countries access to university education is inscribed in the constitution as one of the rights of citizens. This question needs to be analysed within the framework of a reorganization of higher education as a whole, and governments should first make the most of existing structures before planning new ones.

A plan to train tertiary-level staff should be put in place as a matter of urgency, with special attention to current and future needs, the major linkages to be established, the level of training, training cycles and career progression. It should also define terms for the provision of facilities which would enable African universities themselves to train staff and suggest measures for making academic careers attractive. Such a plan should include criteria for assessing and promoting lecturers. And to raise the quality of education, such criteria should bear on *all* the functions of lecturers, that is encompassing the conduct of classes and not only scholarly publications, as is done at present.

Strategies for the Promotion of the Quality of Higher Education in Africa

As indicated, the quality of higher education in Africa has been deteriorating perceptibly, particularly as a result of the extremely rapid increase of student populations, the stagnant development of academic infrastructures, inadequate qualified human and material resources, scientific equipment and teaching materials.

In reaction, African governments and regional higher education organizations on the continent have adopted strategies to regionalize training and to promote the mobility of lecturers and students within a framework of centres of excellence and institutional networks.

Regionalization of Training Institutions

African governments often face extreme difficulties in mobilizing the critical mass of human resources and equipment needed to ensure quality training in certain priority areas. This has impelled regional groupings of political and economic communities to establish common university institutions designed as centres of excellence.

The Common Organisation for Africa and Malagasy (OCAM) is an example of such a community, having created the Inter-state School of Science Veterinary Medicine in Dakar, Senegal; the Inter-state School for Hydraulic Engineers and Technicians and Rural Equipment in Ouagadougou, Burkina Faso; the African and Mauritian School of Architecture and Town Planning in Lomé, Togo; the African School of Computer Science in Libreville, Gabon; and the African Statistical Institute in Kigali, Rwanda. In general, the funds required for the operation of these institutions come from the contributions of the countries which established the institutions and they also sometimes benefit from financial contributions through international cooperation.

Another example is the Economic Community of the Countries of the Great Lakes (CEPGL) which brings together Burundi, Rwanda and Zaire, and within which courses such as pharmacy and psychology are carried out on a regional basis. CEPGL has also established common institutions of research and training such as the Institute for Research in Agronomy and Zootechnology at Gitega, Burundi, the Institute for Information Sciences and Technology in Kinshasa, Zaire, and networks of thematic research involving not only the universities but also research institutes and centres outside the universities.

These structures have contributed immensely to promoting and improving the quality of higher education in Africa. However, quite apart from the insufficiency of financial resources, the CEPGL programmes are being executed with extreme difficulty, due to changes and political instability in the region.

The desire to promote the quality of higher education was again reaffirmed during the Conference of Chancellors of the universities of the Economic Community of Central Africa, held at the University of Science and Technology at Masuku, Gabon. The conference, which discussed the mobility of lecturers and students and the regionalization of postgraduate and doctorate programmes, took important decisions on the strengthening of cooperation between universities in order to respond better to the requirements of quality training.

Institutional Networks

Another strategy adopted is the creation of research and training networks.

African Network of Scientific and Technological Institutions (ANSTI)
This network, established in 1980, is based at the UNESCO regional bureau in Nairobi. Its main objective is to promote cooperation among institutions offering doctorate courses and engaging in research in science and technology.

By 1987 ANSTI had already established three networks linking thirty science faculties, thirty-nine faculties of applied science, and four research institutes. It conducts doctorate programmes in the different participating faculties. Presently, the network is faced with serious problems due notably to inadequate funding. This has prevented it from obtaining the absolutely essential minimum of equipment, scientific infrastructure and human resources needed for training students, and the network is also unable to monitor and evaluate its activities.

The African Regional Postgraduate Programme in Insect Sciences (ARPIS)
This programme was established in 1983 and links twenty-one African universities to the International Centre for Insect Physiology and Ecology (ICIPE). Students register at universities participating in the network but pursue their courses and research work at ICIPE, where they are trained by researchers specialized in the given area, and can make use of laboratory and other facilities at the Centre. By 1992 the programme had produced eighty-six students at doctorate level and ten at master's degree level.

African Consortium for Research in Economics
The Consortium was established in 1988 in Nairobi. It finances and coordinates research activities at departments of economics at African universities. In 1991 it awarded thirty-seven scholarships worth nearly half a million US dollars, subsidized research and publications and disbursed subsidies to finance twenty-one doctoral dissertations. Currently, the Consortium is engaged in setting up three master's degree programmes, one for anglophone universities other than Nigeria, one for Nigeria, and one for francophone universities, with funds from the African Capacity Building Foundation.

The Association of African Universities (AAU)
The Association of African Universities contributes to promoting and raising the quality of higher education in Africa through a range of activities:

- *Setting up common training programmes at the doctorate degree level*
  Several institutions which have indicated their interest in organizing common research and training programmes at the doctoral level need financial assistance to carry out detailed feasibility studies to do the preliminary work, hold the consultations necessary for working out the training programmes, regulations, administrative and legal framework, and distribution of responsibilities.

  The Association is providing this financial assistance and help to design and plan the common programmes, and starting with feasibility studies on establishing a regional training structure for research in environmental sciences.

- *Exchange programme for lecturers and external examiners*
  Under this programme the AAU finances teaching and research missions among African universities. It also bears the expenses of lecturers travelling from one university to another to serve as external examiners, and as members of examining or doctoral dissertation boards, and it pays the travelling expenses of some lecturers and researchers invited to present papers at scientific meetings organized by member universities.

- *Research fellowships and laboratory equipment programmes*
  Within the framework of its Food and Nutrition programme financed by the European Economic Community, the AAU has awarded fellowships to African lecturers and researchers and equipped a number of laboratories. The objective is to facilitate the mobility of African researchers, particularly by enabling them to use available equipment to carry out research work within the framework of the thematic networks. Besides, as part of training of trainers, the Association will grant twenty-five research fellowships every year from 1993 to 1996, to students at doctorate level to enable them to prepare and defend dissertations/theses in recognized priority areas.

- *Establishment and operation of a Pan-African Network of University Pedagogy*
  The AAU has successfully organized three workshops on the improvement of university pedagogy. The third workshop, organized in collaboration with UNESCO in December 1990 at the University of Science and Technology at Masuku, Gabon, led to the establishment of a Pan-African Network of University Pedagogy, the main objective of which was to promote and raise the level of teaching at the universities.

  The network will offer initial training in teaching to newly-employed lecturers, further training courses to experienced lecturers, and train lecturers in university pedagogy. Under the main programmes for the 1993–6 period, AAU will play an important role in the operation of this network.

- *Promotion and strengthening of university–productive sector linkages*
  With funds provided by the International Development Research Centre (IDRC), AAU carried out a number of studies on the state of relations

between the university and the productive sector. Reinforced by case studies on nine countries, this work is aimed at promoting the link between university and industry, which are considered indispensable to ensure the quality and relevance of teaching and research programmes, particularly with regard to the applied sciences.

Through the formation of these institutional networks and regional structures, governments and agencies are striving to address the very serious quality issues in African higher education.

Note

1   The author gratefully acknowledges the financial support of the INQAAHE conference organizers, the International Development Research Centre (IDRC) and the Regional Bureau in Dakar which enabled him to participate in the Montreal conference, and to present this paper.

Part 2

Some National Developments

Chapter 5

Quality Control Efforts in Chile

Soledad Ramirez-Gatica

This chapter addresses the changes that have taken place since 1981 in Chilean higher education. In particular, it analyses the implications of the law that created regional universities and allowed new, private, educational institutions to develop. The paper also considers the impact of new regulatory procedures, and the expected outcomes of a proposed new law which will introduce accreditation concepts and processes for all higher education institutions. Much of the information reported derives from a research study sponsored and funded by the Chilean National Council for Science and Technology.

As in many other countries, the concern for quality control in Chilean higher education has come from government. In 1980, legislation changed a system which previously had been very simple, consisting of eight public universities all modelled on the University of Chile in Santiago. The regional campuses of two of these universities were upgraded, increasing the number of autonomous institutions to eighteen, and allowing new private universities to be established. Post-secondary education was divided into technical education centres, professional institutes, and universities, with only the latter able to grant academic degrees and offer any of twelve named professional programs. All private universities were subject to a regulation procedure called 'examination', whereby a new institution (the examinee) was required to submit its academic programs for approval by one of the autonomous institutions, which also was responsible for student assessment for at least five years.

In 1990, 'accreditation' was introduced for all new institutions, although those working under the previous examination mode could still choose to remain with this if they preferred. Now a further reform requiring accreditation for all institutions regardless of their age or origin, is being considered. The examination, accreditation and new accreditation processes are described here, drawing on the findings of a national study of these quality control efforts. This study was sponsored and funded by the Chilean National Council for Science and Technology.

Examination

The examination process emerged from the need to regulate the performance of the many new private institutions created after 1980. The legislators intended that this would not only ensure the academic quality of the new universities, but would also provide an opportunity to establish collaborative links on a regular basis between the two institutions involved. However, after twelve years of experience it seems that instead of leading to academic exchange, the examination procedure was generally a 'control process' without much room for innovation and creativity in the new universities. There was little concern with research, facilities, or other activities in the examined institution; attention was concentrated only on the approval of programs of studies and the assessment of student achievement.

The national study revealed no general policy framework, with each examiner institution establishing its own mechanisms. Sometimes within the same institution, there were different procedures to regulate the same examination process; in some institutions the process was regulated in detail, with written norms and specifications, whereas elsewhere these were absent. Nevertheless, the system did trigger academic exchange between some institutions, and in some cases collaboration continued even after the examination agreement ceased, in the form of joint research projects, academic exchanges and faculty development activities. Some students were able to apply for transfer or to undertake studies at the examiner institution, and when distance was not a problem, the use of university facilities and equipment by both institutions was facilitated.

A major shortcoming was that most of the activity concentrated on the student examinations which are held at the end of the semester, at a very busy period for all institutions. The examining committees had to assess their own students and then go to the examinee institution to do the same. Many times the only method used was multiple-choice tests, even in subjects where the most appropriate way to measure achievement was through essay papers.

It was found that some of the new private universities, anxious to speed up the approval of new programs, simply copied them from the examiner institution's to circumvent possible delays in modifications or further analysis. This prevented the new institution from preparing innovative programs more fitted to present circumstances and closer to their own identity. And some of the examining faculties declared they perceived some sort of 'preconditioning' in student answers, giving the impression of prior coaching and rote learning.

Nevertheless, this first effort to introduce a higher education quality control mechanism did have the advantage of providing a context of evaluation to the newborn institutions. They were made aware of the need to be accountable for what they did.

Accreditation

In March 1990, the amplified educational law gave full responsibility to the Council of Education (CSE) for implementing, for the first time, a process of accreditation. All new institutions of higher education, at all three levels, have to submit an institutional proposal stating their mission, goals and the means available to reach those goals, including facilities, human resources and target student population. Following CSE approval, the institution remains under the supervision of the CSE for a six-year period to demonstrate the implementation of its institutional plan.

To carry out its duties, the Council calls on academic peers from different parts of the country, faculty members distinguished both within their own universities and at the national level. They scrutinize new programs of study, act as referees in evaluating institutional proposals and take part as visiting teams to verify that what was proposed is being accomplished. Once the six-year period has expired, the new institution becomes autonomous, unless the Council decides to extend the supervision for five more years. Since supervision is limited to the early life of an institution, it is actually closer to the North American concept of 'licensing' than to accreditation as practiced in the USA.

As part of the research study, a questionnaire was sent to evaluators seeking views on the nature of their task, their criteria for judgment, and the main areas for investigation. Almost all saw their task as verifying the congruence between the institution's proposals and what was actually happening. In the absence of any pre-set standards or quality indicators, and lacking previous experience, they tended to evaluate the institution under scrutiny by comparing it with their own. They emphasized that they were as interested in the quality and relevance of resources as in their quantity. In their view, the visit should consider the process of instruction and of research (if any), and the organizational structure and the role played by each person charged with the administration of the institution. More specifically, they were interested in faculty résumés, levels of student achievement and attrition, student services, detailed programs of studies, and the number of library books actually available compared with those listed in the course references. There was no reference to the relationship between the institution and its immediate environment, perhaps reflecting the fact that many of these new private institutions have been established as business enterprises, rather than in response to community need.

The main criteria used by the evaluators were their own internal perceptions, based on their professional experience and personal values. The majority believed that attention should focus on the new institution's processes rather than its results. To that end, they read all official documents, interviewed faculties and students, observed some classes. Apart from one respondent they did not attempt to assess the impact the institution had on the local community, neither did they see themselves as helpers or facilitators of the institution. They perceived their role as evaluator rather than consultant. During 1993, the Council published a set of academic standards which are providing a helpful frame of reference for both evaluators and evaluated.

After the visit, the team writes a report, sometimes with recommendations regarding weak aspects perceived during the visit. This report is submitted to the Council with all the collected information. The institution has sight of the report and is given 10–15 days to submit a response. The Council then issues an official statement regarding the institution's performance: this is confidential (as is the rest of the process), unless the institution itself chooses to disclose the information.

Accreditation is proving to be more comprehensive than the examination process, yet it does not exclude the latter. It is academic-centered, and financial aspects are not given high priority. There is still a need to encourage institutional commitment to the local community; this is specially relevant at this time in Chilean history when the movement towards regional identity and decentralization is growing stronger.

The New Accreditation

These accreditation activities are beginning to provide some public assurance that an institution has academic credibility and is operating according to a minimum set of standards. Now legislation is proposed for new accreditation to cover all institutions regardless of their age. This is intended to be a systematic process geared to the search for excellence; it is to be voluntary, and also public. It is thus very similar to the American concept of accreditation, but with one significant difference: in the USA it is administered by academia itself, whereas in Chile it is to be administered by the Council of Higher Education, an autonomous entity with representatives from the state universities, the private autonomous universities and institutes, the National Council for Science and Technology, the Chilean Supreme Court and the Armed Forces, chaired by the Secretary of Education and financed by the Chilean government.

Conclusion

The main characteristic of Chilean higher education is its diversity. It is heterogeneous from level to level and within each level. It has neither a tradition nor a culture of evaluation within the older institutions; at present, only the new private universities are under continuous scrutiny. However, there is a growing demand for quality assurance for *all* higher education, from the government and from the general public, partly because of financial retrenchment but also because the large institutional offering through the private sector is proving to be competitive, creative and above all responsible. Since Chile has played a leading role in Latin American education, many are observing the experience and results of its efforts in this field.

Chapter 6

Setting up the Danish Centre

Christian Thune

A Centre for Quality Assurance and Evaluation of Higher Education was established by the Danish Ministry of Education and Research and began operating on 1 July 1992. Here the political context for this development is reviewed and the Centre's procedures and methodology are outlined.

The Political Context

The Danish higher education system consists of thirteen universities and university-level institutions and a large number of non-university institutions, many specializing in the health sciences. It has traditionally been subject to a high degree of central steering. Budgets were set according to standard ratios set by the Ministry of Education and allocated at faculty level. The Ministry controlled the form and content of study programmes in considerable detail, and strictly enforced entry quotas in areas where there was heavy student demand. Scrutiny of the quality of process and output was less intense. The Ministry primarily put its trust in its appointed corps of external examiners, who sat in on and co-graded individual examinations. Since 1992, the examiners are also required to make a general report on study programmes.

In 1990, under the slogan 'An Open Market for Education' the then liberal Minister of Education launched an ambitious programme to modernize the higher education sector. This introduced a new study structure with greater student choice. Students are being encouraged to view their studies as modular, tailoring their course to their individual aims with regard to professional profile, quality and level. Institutions have more freedom to decide which programmes to offer, with open enrolment in as many areas as possible. Movement between courses and institutions is being liberalized and the possibilities for credit transfer increased and clarified. This freer mobility is intended to encourage students to make heavier demands on teaching quality. If they are not satisfied, they should supposedly move to an institution with a better reputation. In the words of the Ministry it is thus possible for students as users to 'vote with their feet and shift between institutions', which will then be judged by their student intake and completion rates. In this context, fears are voiced that some institutions will try to meet the new criterion of 'productivity' by lowering standards and requirements.

At the same time, the Ministry is decentralizing — from detailed control to control of overall frameworks and goals. A central element in this is the new law approved by Parliament in 1992, giving presidents and deans considerable prerogatives, and reducing the power of university boards and committees. The challenge of achieving successful decentralization while maintaining programme quality pointed up the need for an organized and systematic evaluation effort.

The Danish Centre

The growing international interest in quality issues has not been greatly reflected within the Danish institutions of higher education, and the initiative for introducing evaluations and quality assurance came from the Committee of Chairmen of the Danish Education Councils. From 1989, the Education Councils on Natural Sciences, Social Sciences and Technical Sciences have undertaken large-scale evaluations of disciplines which were represented at several institutions — covering chemistry, business economics, accounting, geology and electronic engineering — very much along the lines of what was perceived as 'the Dutch model'.

The workload involved soon went far beyond the capacity of the very small secretariat of the Committee of Chairmen, and the Committee decided to support an earlier proposal from the Ministry to set up an independent evaluation agency. The Committee believed that such an independent central body would make it possible to promote the professionalism and legitimacy, which are important requirements for quality improvement. Although the Danish Rectors' Conference did not support the idea, in late 1991 the Danish Parliament established an Evaluation Centre. By mid-1992 the Centre was in business. Its mandate is to initiate evaluation processes, to develop appropriate methods for assessing programmes, to inspire and guide institutions in matters of evaluation and quality, and to compile information on national and international experiences.

Four essential premises were laid down. First the activities of the Centre must focus solely on teaching programmes. Despite the university conviction that research and teaching quality are closely linked, there had been a strong trend towards the separate administration of education and research: a separate advisory committee on research had with the approval of the Ministry taken upon itself to initiate large-scale research evaluations, starting with the health sciences, and this was further complicated by the appointment in January 1993 by a Minister responsible for research and technology.

Secondly, after lengthy considerations it was decided that evaluations should not be voluntary. Despite the general ministerial policy of decentralization, the decisive argument became the need for comprehensive, consistent and systematic evaluations. Thirdly, the Centre cannot offer any financial compensation on the grounds that resources invested by the institution in the self-studies will bring their own reward in terms of assuring quality development, although the work of the Centre would undoubtedly be eased if some financial support were allowed. Finally, it was decided that the Board of the Centre should for the time being be identical to the Committee of Chairmen of the Education Councils.

By the end of 1993 the Centre was staffed by six academics, two secretaries and ten part-time project assistants, and had concluded the first four evaluations, including history and building engineering. During 1994 a further ten evaluations will be undertaken. The Centre covers the thirteen universities and university-level institutions, and a very substantial number of non-university institutions, especially within the health sector. The plan is to complete a full cycle of evaluations by 1998.

Procedures

The Centre has decided to concentrate on the evaluation of programmes rather than whole institutions. It aims to carry out large-scale evaluations of already well-established study programmes on a rotating basis every five years. It also undertakes small-scale *ad hoc* evaluations of trial programmes, and of programmes where acute problems concerning quality have arisen. Although the Ministry tends to focus on quality control, the Centre's mandate clearly includes quality assurance and development, which are more attractive to the higher education institutions. The Centre's task is to create a credible balance between the two.

Three interested parties may request an evaluation: the Education Councils, the Ministry of Education, or the higher education institutions themselves. In fact, all the initial evaluations have been requested by the Education Councils and none from the Ministry. Recently the Conference of Rectors of the Schools of Social Workers and the Schools of Midwifery have asked to be evaluated.

The Centre has no mandate to assess research but believes it is important that research is included at indicator level when education is reviewed, and vice versa. In close cooperation with the Advisory Council on Research, the Centre hopes to activate a pilot project in 1994, to evaluate psychology in terms of research as well as teaching quality. A special problem is the evaluation of non-university further education, which has a different structure and contains other types of programmes, including those with a strong element of work-based learning, and the Centre is considering how best to proceed with the evaluation of such practical training.

A specific Danish dimension in evaluations is the substantial role given to users in the procedures. The attitudes of students, recent graduates and employers are surveyed intensively. Furthermore, representatives of employers are prominent in the steering committees (see later), and must constitute up to one-third of the corps of external examiners.

Although it is argued that confidentiality encourages a more honest and critical self-evaluation, the Centre views openness as essential, and has decided that its procedures and methods must be known, and all reports published or available.

Methodology

The Steering Committee and Secretariat

A steering committee is responsible for the professional oversight of the evaluation; the quality and integrity of its members are crucial, and the Chairman must be perceived by all concerned as credible and authoritative. As a general rule, the Centre tries to recruit to the steering committee at least two prominent employers of graduates from the programme. Composing a group that is representative, authoritative and operational, with an effective Chairman can prove a difficult task. The conduct of the evaluation exercises places heavy demands on the Secretariat, requiring both administrative efficiency and a considerable degree of professionalism.

The Self-study

The primary purpose of the self-study is to present relevant and comprehensive written documentation for the steering committee and the expert panel. The Centre holds briefing meetings with those responsible for drafting the documents and provides a standard manual suggesting that coverage should include some general aspects of the institution; full details of the programme; information about postgraduate provision; cooperation with other higher education institutions, research agencies and the private sector; the social structure of the student body; the corps of external examiners; and involvement in continuing education activities. Any special characteristics should also be covered such as the amount of part-time teaching, the extent of international study programmes, and any experimental courses.

Ideally the self-study should reflect a subtle balance between qualitative and quantitative data. But there is no doubt that the latter, bordering on performance indicators, causes considerable work and some apprehension, and that Danish institutions are as yet unfamiliar with compiling and delivering that kind of information.

A second and perhaps more important purpose of the self-study is to provide the institution and the study programme with a commitment, and a valid procedure and method to continue its own process of quality assurance. In the long-term, the effort invested in the self-studies is less concerned with the delivery of material for a control process, than with local quality improvement.

The Visiting Team of Peers

The experts appointed for the visiting teams need a thorough understanding and knowledge of the subject matter under scrutiny, and they must be independent of the programme and institution being evaluated. The latter is difficult to obtain with the use of national experts, but an international group may not have the local knowledge and understanding; the Centre has resolved this by involving Nordic experts. Although the panel must be independent, its composition must be compatible with, and have no prior bias concerning, the institution under evaluation. The visiting panel consists of at least the chairman of the steering committee supplemented by three to four further external members. This ensures that the steering committee itself has first-hand evidence from the visit, when it approves the final report of the evaluation.

User Surveys

In addition to the material arising from the self-assessment phase and from the external panel, the Centre considers it extremely relevant to integrate user surveys. A survey of students provides some qualitative evaluation with regard to specific parts of the study programme. A survey of recent graduates offers an evaluation of the total study programme and an insight into rates of employment and profiles of positions held by graduates, i.e., the composition of the potential labour market. A survey of employers maps public sector and private industry perceptions of the quality of the study programme and the qualifications of the graduates. These surveys are done by various sampling techniques and are relatively costly. Up to one-third of the budget of an evaluation is tied to reporting on user-attitudes. The Centre is also going to give a report from the external examiners a prominent place in its general procedures.

Report and Follow-up

An evaluation project typically takes up to twelve months from the initiation phase to the submission of the report. Before the final report is published a draft is discussed during a one-day conference, when representatives of institutions and study programmes have an opportunity to comment on or even criticize the premises for the evaluation. The final report is submitted to the relevant Education Council which then takes a position and advises the Ministry of Education on the specific recommendations in the report.

However, the launching of a continuous process of quality assurance is primarily the task of the institution and the study programme, and it is crucial that the institutions themselves are committed to this process. The Centre has little doubt that a series of well executed evaluations do not in themselves bring any merit. The proof of success will be the impact and follow-up in the longer-term, with the foundation for quality improvement launched by a good evaluation. Part of the Centre's mandate is to guide and advise Danish higher education institutions in this context.

Chapter 7

University Accreditation in Korea

Wha-Kuk Lee

This chapter reviews the evolution of Korean university evaluation and accreditation. Its development from 1945 to the present is analysed, with special emphasis on the organization, procedures and criteria of the current accreditation system. Introduced in 1991, this was developed by the Korean Council for University Education and the Korean Ministry of Education, and is largely based on the American accreditation model. Associated contemporary issues and possible modifications to the system are discussed.

Korean higher education has made remarkable progress during the last half century. Today, more than 1.5 million students are enrolled in various higher education institutions (MOE, 1992). In fact Korea is ranked third worldwide, after the USA and Canada, in the number of higher education students per total population, as well as in the percentage of the student age cohort in higher education (UNESCO, 1991).

In preparation for the twenty-first century, the main aim in Korean higher education has been to develop overall excellence in education to complement the massive quantitative expansion that has already taken place. Funding of higher education will be increased, and government policy is being changed from 'control without sufficient support' to 'more support without strong control'. These changes have been welcomed by the universities, and with the agreement of both government and institutions a university accreditation system was introduced in 1991 to ensure accountability.

The Development of the University Evaluation System

While higher education in Korea dates back to 372 AD, modern university education equivalent to that of universities in western countries has only been developed during the last five decades. The modern education system in Korea was established largely under American influence after the Second World War and that is why Korean education resembles the American system and is still very much influenced by it (KCUE, 1990). Today, out of the 151 four-year colleges and universities in Korea, more than 70 per cent of students are enrolled in private institutions. The government in the past did not have the means to support these private institutions financially, yet it exercised the same control over them as over the national universities which received half of their budget from the government. This tight government control over the structure and functions of all universities made both national and private institutions similar in many ways.

The development of university education in relation to evaluation and accreditation evolved through five stages; *laissez-faire* (1945–1953), government control (1954–1972), Experimental Colleges (1973–1981), KCUE and institutional self-evaluation (1982–1991), and university accreditation (1992–).

Laissez-faire 1945–1953

When the Japanese occupation ended in 1945, the inherent Korean thirst for learning soon revived. This combined with the beginning of a post-war baby boom led to the rapid expansion of higher education institutions. As government funds were stretched to the limit with post-war economic reconstruction, many private universities were established to meet the growing demand. In spite of the Korean War from 1950 to 1953, higher education continued to expand, but no formal university evaluation system was introduced.

Government Control 1954–1972

By the end of the Korean War in 1953, the government was able to look carefully at the development and planning of higher education. In 1952 a Presidential Decree had already been passed for the enforcement of the Education Law which was to provide a legal basis for control over universities. The most urgent problem was the assignment of student quotas to colleges and universities. In 1955, there were further attempts to regulate higher education with the promulgation of another Presidential Decree which set standards for the establishment of colleges and universities. But these attempts to rationalize the system failed because of the inconsistent application of higher education policies and the excessively strong demand for higher education.

The situation was further complicated by a student revolution in 1960 against the dictatorial government of the day which led to the establishment of the Second Republic. With this civilian government, there was a movement to democratize education. However, before any changes could be implemented, a military coup occurred and in 1961 the Third Republic was set up. The general view of this military government was that universities were the main threat to social order and the source from which the destabilization of society could occur. Consequently, government control over the higher education system was tightened by scaling down student quotas and through the introduction of a degree registration system. In short, university evaluation during this time took the form of investigation and audit *after* the problems had occurred.

Experimental Colleges 1973–1981

By 1971, Korea was rapidly becoming a developed nation. With industrialization and modernization, the government determined that higher education should be more closely geared towards meeting the needs of national development, and a strategy for the selective support of institutions on the basis of educational excellence was devised. Pilot colleges were given more financial support and a greater measure of autonomy. The 'Experimental College' project, as it came to be called, included selection of students by certain fields and colleges rather than to departments, the reduction of graduation credits from 160 to 140, and the introduction of minor and double-major sequences. It was particularly significant that these changes had been designed by the government but in cooperation with university educators. While these changes were not wholly successful and were subsequently abolished, the tradition of faculty participation in university evaluation had been established.

KCUE and Institutional Self-evaluation 1982–1991

During the 'Experimental College' period, the expansion of higher education had slowed down and this led to a rapid increase in the number of 'repeaters' taking college entrance examinations. This came to be a major social problem, which the Fifth Republic government determined to overcome by greatly expanding the higher education system. Simultaneously there was a growing realization within Korean universities of the need for more autonomy, if universities were really to fulfil their educational mission. The Ministry of Education (MOE), also recognized the need for the higher education system to become more democratic. So a plan was devised for an intermediate organization to be established, and in 1982 the Korean Council for University Education (KCUE) was founded.

KCUE became an inter-university organization made up of all four-year colleges and universities in Korea. In 1984, the KCUE Act was promulgated and through this Act the government empowered KCUE to evaluate its member institutions (KCUE, 1992a) at both institutional and program level. Institutional evaluation was carried out in five-year cycles and various program evaluations were performed on a yearly basis; the evaluation results were not made public.

Thus over the last five decades, considerable progress has taken place in the development of a university evaluation system. Initially, after the Korean War, the government controlled the system and then during the 'Experimental College' period, both educators and the government started to work cooperatively together for the improvement of higher education. With universities themselves more in control of their own destinies than ever before, the need to develop a sound and democratic evaluation and accreditation system is now being addressed.

University Accreditation 1992–

After the establishment of the Sixth Republic, Korean society democratized more rapidly. Efforts to reform the education system accelerated and there were fresh demands for more democracy and autonomy in higher education. Out of this came the Presidential Commission for Education Reform which carried out its work from 1985 to 1988. One of the key recommendations of the Commission was that a formal accreditation system should be introduced. The government accepted the recommendations of the Commission and debate followed about the nature, structure and functions of accreditation. The government wanted to introduce both program and institutional accreditation simultaneously, but KCUE argued that it was too soon to introduce a total system. Finally, a compromise was reached so that from 1991 program accreditation was to take place with institutional accreditation being postponed until 1996.

By October 1991, preparations were made for the first accreditation of departments of physics and electronic engineering. Self-evaluation was carried out by each of these departments in the universities concerned from January to June 1992 and then on-site visits took place during July and August. The results were analysed at KCUE by the end of 1992, and lists of universities with sound departments were announced in March 1993. The second year of accreditation, focused on departments of chemistry and mechanical engineering.

The Current University Accreditation System

Who should do the accrediting? What standards should be used? How should the process be undertaken? The nature of the accrediting organization and its standards and procedures are briefly described here.

The Accrediting Organization

Initially, the system was managed by MOE and KCUE with the role of accreditation shared. Within MOE, there was an Advisory Council for University Education Policy which made recommendations on matters of university accreditation to the Minister who made the final decision. However, in 1993, MOE and KCUE established an independent accrediting body within the KCUE called the Council for University Accreditation (KCUA) to act as the highest authority on university evaluation. This Council is composed of sixteen representatives from the university, industry and government.

Standards of Accreditation

Departments within a subject area are evaluated and the standards of accreditation are prepared on the basis of six major categories, each with

Table 3: Structure of Accreditation Standards for Departments of Physics

Major Category	Subcategory	Number of Evaluation Items Undergrad.	Grad.
1. Objectives of department	1.1 Contents of objectives	3	–
	1.2 Implementation of objectives	4	2
	1.3 Design of objectives	4	1
	1.4 Realization of objectives	4	2
2. Curriculum	2.1 Structure of curriculum	8	6
	2.2 Improvement of curriculum	5	5
	2.3 Contents of curriculum	5	5
	2.4 Instruction	5	2
	2.5 Laboratory work	3	–
	2.6 Assessment	3	3
3. Students	3.1 Admission of students	4	2
	3.2 Student guidance	5	2
	3.3 Student activities	5	–
	3.4 Student welfare	4	5
	3.5 Quality of graduates	4	3
4. Faculty	4.1 Employment	5	–
	4.2 Organization of faculty	7	3
	4.3 Teaching loads	5	7
	4.4 Faculty development	3	–
	4.5 Faculty research	–	8
5. Facilities	5.1 Building	14	5
	5.2 Equipment	13	9
6. Administration and Finance	6.1 Administration	6	2
	6.2 Finance	6	4
Total		125	76

subcategories and separate evaluation questions which may vary slightly for different subjects. The major categories are: objectives, curriculum, students, faculty, facilities, and administration and finance (KCUE, 1991). Table 3 shows the structure of standards used for departments of physics (KCUE, 1992b).

For each subcategory some evaluation questions such as 'Has the curriculum been improved during the last five years?' are seeking qualitative information; others, for example, 'What is the average teaching load of faculty members in the department?' are to obtain quantitative information. For each evaluation item, three criteria are assigned to identify good(A), moderate(B), and poor(C) departments. For example, for the item 'What is the rate of doctoral degree holders among faculty members?' (A) is over 90 per cent, (B) 70–80 per cent and (C) below 70 per cent. 'A' counts as 1.0 and 'B' and 'C' are 0.7 and 0.4 respectively. The score of any one item is calculated by multiplying the result by a weighting for that item. By summing up the score of each item in each major subcategory, the total score for any one department is obtained.

Accreditation Procedures

The key stages in the accreditation of a department are self-evaluation study, review of the self-study report, an on-site visit, and announcement of the results. The Council for University Accreditation within the KCUE decides which departments will be evaluated, then KCUE consults with professional associations related to the departments to be evaluated and organizes an accreditation committee made up of university academics. This committee develops the standards and criteria for accreditation and the departments in all the universities involved carry out a self-evaluation study based on these within six months. Then the self-study report is sent to KCUE and the accreditation committee.

The review of the self-study involves reading the report and making evaluations as well as identifying questions needed to collect additional information during the on-site visit. An on-site visit team of three academics spends one whole day evaluating a department, and its report is sent to the department. Based on the marks given for each evaluation item, KCUE calculates the scores of each major category and the total score for the individual department, and then classifies all the departments evaluated into three groups: good, moderate and poor. The results of the on-site evaluation are reported to the KCUA, and following Council deliberation a list of good departments is announced.

Issues in University Accreditation

With the first trial of departmental accreditation in 1991–2, many anticipated and unanticipated problems came to light. Despite adaptation to this US style of accreditation, profound cultural differences still emerged. The most important difference between the Korean and the American system is that the latter is non-governmental and voluntary whereas the former is government-initiated and non-voluntary. This raises five issues that are important to Korea, and could be of common concern to universities internationally.

Goals of Accreditation

In the United States, the main goal of accreditation is to ensure a minimum quality of education. KCUE agrees, but MOE wants to use the accreditation process to select the departments and universities for increased financial support and a greater measure of autonomy. MOE's position is that the departments and universities selected will become examples for the other universities to follow, and that by this means the poorer universities will be pushed into improving their performance. KCUE's view is that this will lead to a vicious circle whereby universities that are evaluated as 'poor' would never have sufficient funding or sufficient self-determination to improve. KCUE's argument is that the poorer universities need to get more support from the government after evaluation. So while MOE and KCUE agree that the ultimate goal of accreditation is to promote excellence in higher education, there is disagreement about how this goal is to be accomplished. KCUE argues this case using a Korean proverb as an analogy, 'If we bite the small fingers it hurts just the same as when we bite the big fingers.' In other words, the smaller fingers are as important as the big fingers.

The Accrediting Organization

KCUE is composed of the four-year higher education institutions in Korea. So in performing the tasks of evaluation, it is evaluating its own member institutions, and the government and some educators remained uncertain about the objectivity and reliability of the evaluation. However, KCUE believed the involvement of MOE to be inappropriate because university evaluation must be non-governmental. This problem has been overcome by the establishment of a third independent body, the Council for University Accreditation, although the management of the actual accreditation activities will continue to be carried out by the Department of University Evaluation at KCUE because of the expertise it has accumulated in the past.

Who Should Be Accredited?

Should undergraduate and graduate programs be evaluated together or separately? Should the evaluation be of departments or academic fields? The problem is that within the university education system in Korea, there are more than 500 types of departments and many of these are quite similar. If mechanical engineering is going to be evaluated for example, then there is a dozen different types of departments that should be evaluated. There are also special problems involved with evaluating the undergraduate programs in these departments, because early specialization is not considered desirable. If all 500 were to be evaluated in a decade, fifty types of department should be covered every year. Some argue for evaluation by fields rather than departments. However, departmental evaluation is easier to manage and less costly, so the KCUE Committee for University Evaluation has recommended the following priorities for the selection of departments to be accredited:

- departments in the fields of science and engineering required for the promotion of national industry and economy;
- departments that will lead industrial and technical development towards the twenty-first century;
- departments which offer licenses in technical specialities;

- departments established in more than ten universities; and
- departments of a university established more than five years ago.

With these priorities, the number of departments to be evaluated can be reduced to less than 100. But still the problem remains only partially solved, because not all departments can be evaluated straight away.

Should accreditation be compulsory? There are many arguments for and against voluntary and non-voluntary accreditation. At present, a non-voluntary system has been adopted, but the Council for University Accreditation is to review this in the near future.

Standards and Criteria

Firstly, there is involved here the traditional argument as to whether to evaluate input, process and output of university education, or some combination of these? And it is indeed difficult to organize these three factors into criteria. Should the criteria then be value-rated for the evaluation of the current situation or future directions or both? At present, standards of evaluation are divided into six major categories. Should the category scores be combined into one grand score in order to rank the universities? And indeed, should this judgment be made in the first place? The universities are strongly against judgment being made on the basis of a total score. Should the criteria for private and national universities be the same or different, given the major differences in government financial support between the two sectors?

The Use of Results

And lastly, should the results be made public or not? Some of those associated with accreditation argue that the results must be publicized because accreditation itself implies that the results are made public to the society. Without publication, they contend, this process would not contribute to the development of university education. There is also the view that publication could cause student demonstrations, thus retarding the development of university education. Both arguments have validity, and so the problem still remains. In the context of the last decade, during which none of KCUE's evaluation results have been publicized, experience suggests the need to publish evaluation results for them to be truly effective.

Conclusion

There is agreement that Korea needs university accreditation, but getting agreement about the detailed working of the system has been where most problems have emerged. In the past, Korea adopted the American education system and within it a certain brand of university education. In the longer-term, what is sought is a Korean accreditation system for higher education that will specifically meet local needs. This is a crucial challenge that faces the whole of Korean university society today.

References

MOE (1992) *Statistical Yearbook of Education*, Ministry of Education, Republic of Korea, Seoul.

KCUE (1990) *Korean Higher Education: Its Development, Aspects and Prospects*, Korean Council for University Education, Seoul.

KCUE (1991) *Handbook for the Accreditation of Academic Department (in Korean)*, Korean Council for University Education, Seoul.

KCUE (1992a) *Korean Council for University Education 1992–1993*, Korean Council for University Education, Seoul.

KCUE (1992b) *Standards and Criteria for the Accreditation of Department of Physics (in Korean)*, Korean Council for University Education, Seoul.

UNESCO (1991) *1990 Statistical Yearbook*, UNESCO, Paris.

Chapter 8

The Work of the New Zealand Qualifications Authority

Alan Barker

The development of National Qualifications Framework and the establishment of the New Zealand Qualifications Authority to coordinate and provide quality assurance for all secondary and tertiary-level qualifications is described. The author summarizes the procedures for setting the standards for units and degrees within the framework, accrediting institutions to deliver the units, and moderation of provision.

Background

The New Zealand Qualifications Authority (NZQA) was established under the Education Amendment Act in July 1990 with a brief to develop a comprehensive and coherent framework for all nationally recognized qualifications.

Previously, the New Zealand qualifications system had been confusing and complex. Few qualifications linked with each other and in some learning areas there were no nationally recognized qualifications at all. It was difficult, to say the least, for people to obtain the skills necessary for their chosen career and even more difficult for people wanting to change direction or retrain. There was little scope for the recognition of prior learning and skills. In addition, there were discrepancies and inconsistencies in nomenclature and variance in the setting and delivery of standards.

A number of factors contributed to the need for an integrated qualifications' system, including: high unemployment particularly in the 18–25 year age group; increasing retention rates in secondary schools but low participation rates in post-compulsory education and training; an emphasis on upskilling to increase international competitiveness; and the lack of qualifications in the current workforce. All this, alongside the rapid rate of technological change and a new Industry Skills Strategy outlined in the Industry Training Act 1992, and within a context of greater accountability for education spending and 'customer pays' education.

The result of a decade of debate was a National Qualifications Framework. This aims to provide the base for a coordinated, coherent, flexible, post-compulsory education and training sector. It will incorporate on-job training and recognize prior learning and will provide a continuum of learning opportunities through the adoption of a modular approach. It will also end the traditional binary division created by separate education and training systems, which has led to two different qualifications' systems with rigid distinctions between providers, and an enduring perception that the vocational is second-class.

The move to a unit standard format, signals a shift in emphasis from the traditional focus on inputs and content, to a focus on outcomes where learners must demonstrate specified skills, knowledge and competencies. Each unit standard will have clearly defined learning outcomes. The unit standards will cover general and vocational education and produce a single, comprehensive system.

The Framework establishes the parameters for significant change to occur. Three of its fundamental principles are that learning is a life-long process, that all learning is significant, and that higher education does not take place only within universities, and is not reserved to 'academic' subjects.

There are eight levels to the Framework encompassing National Certificate (levels 1–4) and National Diplomas (levels 5–7). Initial degrees will also be placed at level 7; other degrees, higher certificates and diplomas will be placed at level 8. The quality assurance systems of the NZQA are intended to apply equally across all levels of the Framework from senior secondary level through to doctoral degrees.

Quality Assurance

The NZQA's role is to coordinate all these secondary school and tertiary-level qualifications, so that they have a purpose and relationship to one another that the public, employers and students can understand. It must also ensure that quality assessment and improvement operates throughout the system in the development and approval of qualifications, the accreditation of providers, and the verification of assessment standards. Six of the Authority's twelve legislative functions either directly or indirectly authorize quality assurance mechanisms.

NZQA is adopting an unequivocal commitment to achieving quality through a five-stage process:

- registration of private training establishments;
- setting the standards by unit registration or (degree) course approval;
- accreditation (ensuring that the provider has the capacity to deliver the standards);
- moderation (ensuring that the standards have been delivered and that they are consistent between providers); and
- audit (an independent evaluation of the whole system).

Alan Barker

Registration of Private Training Establishments

The Authority registers private training establishments to ensure that basic educational and consumer safeguards are met, and this is a pre-requisite to accreditation. The registration process includes an appraisal of an institution's organizational and educational management, its legal basis, financial management, purpose and goals, its premises, quality assurance and quality control mechanisms, and its long-term potential. Once a private training establishment is operational, evaluation is ongoing.

There is no such registration process for existing state providers (tertiary institutions and schools) since the responsibility for their success lies with the state through the Ministry of Education and tertiary institution's Councils. The criteria which the state providers must meet is already clearly defined in current legislation.

Setting the Standards: Units

Unit standards are the nationally registered outcome statements (elements) and assessment criteria. They are the building blocks of the National Qualifications Framework. Qualifications will consist of unit standards which are linked and interchangeable, and have been determined by standards-setting bodies consisting of representatives from industry, the academic community and relevant professional groups. Learners may study one unit standard or a combination of unit standards leading to a qualification. They can cross-credit unit standards between qualifications where appropriate and between places of learning.

Unit standards vary in size and each unit standard will have its own credit rating depending on the value ascribed by the standards-setting body. Each credit equates with 10–12 learner hours for the average student, with a maximum of 120 credits for any one unit standard.

Accredited providers will be free to develop learning programmes around unit standards. It is envisaged that there will be considerable scope to develop individual styles of delivery so long as the learning outcomes are achieved. Rather than dictating in any way how a unit standard or group of unit standards is taught, the Authority is seeking to encourage innovative approaches.

This standard-setting process must be open and clear, and allow all those who use the standards to have an input. As part of this process NZQA is establishing partnerships with providers, teachers, students, industry and other user groups to ensure that there is joint responsibility for setting and maintaining quality. This approach is consistent with the recent reform of education administration and the devolution of management decisions to schools and tertiary institutions.

The Qualifications Authority has been a catalyst in the planning and coordination of standards-setting groups. The groups that set, maintain and endorse unit standards will represent all major groups connected with an area, for example forestry or computing or mathematics or history. They will have responsibility for the development, evaluation and endorsement of all unit standards and qualifications in that category. They will be either Industry Training Organizations (ITOs) as defined by the Industry Training Act 1992, or national standards bodies as defined by NZQA.

Although often the users of a standard may be obvious for example in the case of industry, in other instances, particularly in some areas of general education, for example Latin or anthropology, they may be less apparent. In these general areas the academic and research community is seen as the proxy for the general public.

The roles of the standards-setting bodies include:

- analysing the skills and knowledge in their skill area for the development of unit standards and qualifications;
- establishing boundaries and areas of overlap;
- overseeing the development of unit standards in the format required by the Qualifications Authority for registration in the public domain;
- undertaking sufficient consultation to ensure a wide acceptance of the standards;
- agreeing to quality management systems in consultation with the Qualifications Authority to maintain nationally consistent standards, including criteria and a procedure for registered assessors; and
- arranging for the regular review of standards and qualifications to enable a revision or update.

All unit standards need to be approved in the appropriate standards-setting group before being registered onto the Framework by the Qualifications Authority..

Setting the Standards: Degree-course Approval

The standards of degree qualifications offered by polytechnics or private training establishments have to be approved by NZQA, through a process of peer appraisal based on analysis of documentation, followed by a site visit. The peer panel includes two NZQA nominees from the relevant discipline, other academics, and professional business representatives as appropriate (O'Connor, 1993).

Following strongly expressed opposition, it was agreed that the power to approve and moderate degrees within the universities should remain with the Vice-Chancellors' Academic Programmes Committee. However, the Qualifications Authority and the New Zealand Vice-Chancellors' Committee (NZVCC) are using a common set of criteria for evaluation of degree programmes.

Accreditation

The accreditation process involves evaluating a provider's capacity to deliver the unit or course standards. Only an accredited provider is able to offer unit standards and qualifications which are registered on the Framework. Where foreign students are enrolled, providers offering any courses of three-months duration or more must be accredited. Accreditation does not evaluate the actual performance of a provider because this will be appraised when the outcomes of the course are monitored and again when re-accreditation takes place.

Accreditation can only be given to a higher education institution, (university, wananga[1], polytechnic or college of education), a school, a registered private training establishment or a government training establishment. As with course approval, accreditation of universities has been vested in the NZVCC.

In some instances evaluation of written documentation may be sufficient but in others on-site visits may also be required. National standards bodies may choose to be involved directly in accreditation, or may prefer to leave it to the Qualifications Authority; they are expected to aim at ensuring quality while remaining mindful of accreditation (and moderation) costs.

A provider may apply for unit accreditation, group accreditation or general accreditation. *Unit accreditation* involves evaluation of the capacity to deliver the standards contained in a single unit. *Group accreditation* involves evaluation of the capacity to deliver the standards contained within a number of named units. This also enables accreditation for unit standards that may be registered within that part of the database in the future. *General accreditation* recognizes a provider's capacity to deliver all National Certificate and Diploma units within the Framework. This will only be considered when endorsement has been received from all user groups and when evidence of quality delivery has been confirmed through the audit process.

Before a provider is considered for accreditation, the Authority evaluates eight areas:

- teaching programs and systems for their evaluation;
- financial, administrative and physical resources;
- processes for staff selection, appraisal and development;
- systems for establishing and clearly publicizing student entry;
- student guidance and student-support systems;
- integrated arrangements for any off-site practical/work-based components;
- systems for ensuring fair, valid and consistent assessment; and
- channels for providing students with fair and regular feedback and progress reports.

Providers are also required to undertake ongoing evaluation of their policies and procedures as part of their internal quality management.

Moderation

Holders and users of national qualifications must have confidence that different assessors throughout New Zealand have assessed to the same standards.
Moderation of assessment determines that the standards have been delivered
and that they are consistent between providers. It involves targeting selective
representative points to check the quality of the whole and must be specified
at the time of unit registration or course approval.

In the tertiary arena institutions have the freedom 'to teach and assess
students in the manner they consider best promotes learning'. In reality there
is a delicate balance between the responsibilities of tertiary institutions and
those of the Authority. This area of overlap between the legislative functions
of the Authority and the institutional autonomy of tertiary providers is currently the subject of much discussion and negotiation, or in the words of one
Vice-Chancellor 'various degrees of ambiguity and tension' (Malcolm, 1993).

The Authority allows for flexibility in the external moderation process.
It can be either centrally established and directed, or a national moderation
system of local networks. In the first option, the system will be designed
centrally by individual standards-setting bodies and/or their agents who could
include representatives from the Qualifications Authority, a national industry
organization or professional association, an individual provider or consortium
of providers and a private consultant. In the second option, the system will
be designed locally by providers and workplaces and may include representation from local user groups. Alternatively a national standards body may
conclude that expectations can be met through internal moderation without
needing to add external moderation requirements.

Although moderation activities will depend on what each standards body
considers appropriate, the functions will usually be:

- to verify that assessments are fair, valid and consistent and to identify
  where there is any need for redesigning assessment activities, or for
  reassessing students;
- to adjust interpretations of standards for the future;
- to ensure that the assessment decisions made by different assessors are
  within the accepted limits;
- to provide a mechanism for handling assessment appeals; and
- to provide feedback on the quality of unit standards.

Moderation may happen at the start of assessment to examine the design
of activities, marking schedules and achievement targets. Or it can occur
during particular assessments so that moderators can work alongside assessors
where a product is difficult to look at or move, or perhaps lacks durability.
Moderation may also take place after particular assessments to look at the
outputs of an assessment activity, for example, a candidates' work. A random
approach may also be used in the form of sample spot checks of a range of

assessments. The challenge will always be to select the sample that best represents the whole. There may be light, random sampling or it may be more appropriate to focus on assessment decisions made on borderline candidates.

There must not, however, be an intrusion into academic freedom. Although moderation of assessment ensures that assessment is to the required standards it does not examine what is taught or how. Legislation protects the freedom of institutions to assess in the ways they consider best promotes learning. Moderation is the public scrutiny of those ways to ensure that assessment is fair, valid and consistent and these two considerations must be kept in balance.

Audit

The final aspect of the Qualifications Authority's quality assurance program is quality audit, to check on the quality systems which are already in place and to ensure that they comply with a provider's previously stated objectives. If a quality audit does reveal that a local system has weakened and there is no evidence of a strategy to improve the situation, the general accreditation will be withdrawn.

The NZVCC have already set up an Academic Audit Unit which will undertake this function for the universities. Modelled on the lines of the former UK Academic Audit Unit (now part of the UK Higher Education Quality Council), its goal is to provide enhanced accountability by making the quality of academic performance in the universities more transparent while still retaining academic autonomy (Malcolm, 1993).

Indeed it is the Authority's intention that the other quality management functions will progressively be devolved to providers. In addition to those already mentioned as delegated to the NZVCC, the Authority is exploring similar options with the Association of Polytechnics of New Zealand (APNZ). In the school sector, the Education Review Office (ERO) which conducts assurance audits of all contractual arrangements between schools and the state will assist in the quality audit process.

Conclusion

The concept of quality management underpins all of the Qualifications Authority's systems and functions with an unequivocal commitment to quality assurance and improvement. Within New Zealand the move towards devolved responsibility requires that providers and user groups demonstrate a similar commitment. Devolution means that responsibility needs to be shared. Although not all providers will take the same route the principles remain the same.

The NZQA believes that quality will be found where the new skills and knowledge acquired conform accurately to a well-designed specification and where the learning environment is responsive to the needs of all its learners. Where the specification is wrong, the skills and knowledge are incorrectly identified, or where the learning environment does not enable students to meet the standards specified, then quality will not be found.

Note

1 Wananga: A wananga is characterized by teaching and research that maintains, advances and disseminates knowledge and develops intellectual independence, or assists the application of knowledge regarding *ahuatanga* Maori (Maori tradition) according to *tikanga* Maori (Maori custom).

References

MALCOLM, W. (1993) *The Development of an Academic Audit Unit in New Zealand*, Paper presented at the INQAAHE Conference, Montreal, Canada.
O'CONNOR, J. (1993) *Quality Assurance for Degrees Approved by the New Zealand Qualifications Authority*, Paper presented at the INQAAHE Conference, Montreal, Canada.

Chapter 9

A View from Quebec

Claude Hamel

The chapter describes higher education provision in Quebec and the complementary role of the Council of Universities and the Conference of Rectors and Principals in advising the Minister on the need for, and quality of, new programs. The universities have also recently introduced a review system for existing programs along the lines of the UK quality audit mechanisms.

Higher Education in Quebec

In Canada, education is the responsibility of the provinces: there are thus ten systems of higher education, each with its own characteristics. Through the financial agreements between the provinces and the federal government, the latter can intervene, albeit indirectly, by contributing to the financing of higher education. Transfers made under the financial agreements are unconditional, and the provinces can use the funds as they wish. In the area of research, however, through its granting agencies, the federal government plays a major role.

The ten systems of higher education are quite similar, with one exception, Quebec, where, between secondary school and university, there is a third tier, the colleges. The latter contain two major streams: a three-year professional stream, which offers training for the labour force, and a two-year pre-university stream. Most candidates thus arrive at university with eleven years of primary and secondary schooling and two years of collegiate study, although close to 20 per cent of the students who have taken professional training in the colleges also pursue university studies.

At the university, the undergraduate program generally lasts three years, the master's program two, and the doctoral three. In 1992–3, Quebec's university system comprised:

- twenty universities in ten economic regions of Quebec offering over 1,600 undergraduate programs (800 of which are bachelor's programs) and over 700 master's and doctoral programs;
- 254,000 students, 56 per cent of whom are women;
- 215,000 undergraduate and 39,000 graduate students;

- 53 per cent full-time students;
- over 9,500 foreign students from 140 countries;
- over 51,000 new graduates per year;
- over 8,500 professors and about 9,000 lecturers;
- 18,500 members of administrative and support staff;
- around $600 million in research grants;
- operating budget of $2 billion and capital budget of $195 million.

Quebec universities enjoy a great deal of autonomy. Each university determines its own pedagogical regime and develops its own programs of teaching and research. Nevertheless, new bachelor's, master's, and doctoral programs must be approved for budgetary purposes by the Minister for Higher Education and Science. Quebec universities are totally responsible for setting their own requirements regarding admission and registration of students, for granting their own diplomas, hiring staff, and establishing working conditions. At the organizational level, the Ministry intervenes principally by means of the budgetary regulations that govern university financing. Operational grants represent around 87 per cent of university funding and the universities enjoy wide latitude in the use of this money.

Two other organizations are involved in the system as a whole: the Council of Universities and the Conference of Rectors and Principals of Quebec Universities (CREPUQ). The Council acts in an advisory capacity to the Minister on the status and needs of university teaching and research. The Conference of Rectors and Principals unites all Quebec universities, the universities themselves providing funding for the organization. Its role involves coordination and lobbying; it also carries out institutional research and provides services to its members.

Promotion of Quality

It is in this context that Quebec's higher education institutions have designed evaluation mechanisms and devices to improve the quality of their performance. As already indicated, Quebec universities, in accordance with North American tradition, enjoy tremendous autonomy; they carry full responsibility for the design and management of their programs of study and for granting diplomas attesting to competence, knowledge, and skills consonant with the curriculum, although proposed and established programs of study are each subject to specific quality assurance procedures.

Quality Assurance of New Programs of Study

To accomplish their training mission, Quebec universities are responsible for offering programs that provide quality education and respond to the needs of society. Each university has its own internal policies and procedures for developing and approving programs it wishes to set up. Once a new program has been approved internally, the university submits it to CREPUQ for quality evaluation by the Commission for Evaluation of New Programs whose mandate and membership are designed to guarantee autonomy and ensure peer-evaluation. The Commission reviews the prospective program and sends a report back to the university outlining its opinion. On the basis of this, the university decides whether it should make any modifications before transmitting it, accompanied by the Commission's evaluation report, to the Minister. At the Minister's request, the Council of Universities then evaluates the timeliness of the new program. Finally, the Minister, on the basis of the Commission's opinion on quality and the Council's opinion on timeliness, decides whether to authorize establishment of the new program and to grant the necessary financing.

In its documentation the university must explain, among other things, the reasons for creating the program. It must also indicate its goals, showing how the program responds to scientific, socio-economic, cultural, or pedagogical needs, mentioning the prospective clientele, and describing how the program contributes to the development of the university system in terms of establishing new activities or consolidating or refining existing ones. This dossier must also include an outline of the curriculum, the teaching or research activities involved, and the teaching staff and physical and financial resources required or available.

The basis of the Commission's evaluation is that a program's quality depends on the appropriateness of its goals to the means available. The Commission — and the experts whose opinion it invites — carefully examine various aspects of these means to reach its conclusions. The points to be evaluated can be divided into four categories: the framework for the program, training activities, teaching staff, and material resources.

The framework relates to the structures and regulations specific to the establishment. The Commission would like to be certain, for example, that admission criteria ensure that students admitted have the ability and the training necessary to pursue the program's goals; that the number of credits, their sequence by session, and the program of studies will allow the student to achieve these goals by a reasonable progression; that the pedagogical regulations allow for an appropriate method for evaluating student learning; that the program's administrative structure will ensure that students have adequate training.

The Commission considers, for the general undergraduate level and the professional master's level, matters such as basic training, the relative importance of required and elective courses, the balance between theoretical and practical studies, and the sequence of activities. For the research master's and doctoral level, the Commission looks at the relationship between the program and the professors' research activities, links between teaching and research, and supervision of students.

Regarding teaching staff, the Commission carefully examines the qualifications of the individual professors — their degrees, experience, publications, and grants — the characteristics of the teaching staff as a whole, and the qualifications of outside individuals: lecturers, clinical lecturers, those supervising internships, etc. For master's and doctoral programs, the Commission will also take into account the procedures and criteria for approval of professors and researchers who teach and supervise research in the program.

Regarding material resources, the Commission examines whether libraries, computer equipment, laboratories, training centres, and work spaces will provide students with the support they need during the program.

Briefly stated, these are the major elements that form the gist of quality evaluation, and on which the Commission, assisted by outside expertise, bases its decision. For the most part, the Commission's judgments are based on qualitative assessments rather than quantitative parameters. As for procedures, the first step is a preliminary analysis of the proposal, an analysis that most often ends up with a request for further information to clarify some aspects. It often happens that the project does not pass this stage and is returned to the university, which then determines if it should modify the program's content as the Commission suggests.

The Commission names four experts, two of whom are chosen from a list of candidates submitted by the university and two directly by the Commission after consultation with the university. These are generally university academics, recognized experts in their discipline or field of study. They must have no ties with the university concerned and one of the four must come from a university outside Quebec. Their mandate is to analyse the prospective program according to indications supplied by the Commission (taking into account specific questions formulated after the preliminary analysis), to visit the establishment concerned, and to produce a report. The experts are asked to prepare individual rather than joint reports as the Commission wishes to derive maximum benefit from these expert advisers.

In the third stage, the Commission analyses the experts' recommendations. It produces its evaluation report — including its quality assessment — and sends it to the university. The Commission's opinion can be positive and may be accompanied by a number of conditions and suggestions: for example, that the university not mount the program until certain it has the necessary teaching staff, that the university revise the new program's admission requirements, that a certain sequence of courses be reduced and another enriched, etc. Alternatively, the Commission can render a negative opinion on the quality of the program.

In principle, it is up to the university to use the opinion of the Commission as it sees fit. For example, the university may decide that for any number of reasons it is not important to pursue one or more of the conditions in the evaluation report. It then runs the risk of not being granted authorization to implement the new program, especially since the opinion of the Commission commands wide respect. But this possibility remains strictly theoretical, since so far no university has ever decided to go ahead without the Commission's approval.

Another very real possibility exists, and has indeed occurred. A program can receive a favourable judgment on quality from the Commission and an unfavourable judgment on timeliness from the Council of Universities. It is then up to the Minister to make a decision. The university is not necessarily prevented from setting up a program that has no Ministry authorization so long as it will assume the (mainly financial) consequences.

For granting public funds, there is a separate evaluation of the timeliness of supporting a new program. This analysis contains four parts. First of all, the prospective program should respond to clearly defined scientific, socio-economic, cultural, or pedagogical needs. Some programs relate to the development of a discipline; others respond to precise needs in the job market. Still others support research and artistic or literary expression or, through their pedagogical formula, result in a fresh approach. It is essential that this diversity of goals be recognized.

The prospective program should also contribute to the development of Quebec's university system in terms of creating new activities, or consolidating or refining existing ones. For example, it may complete a broad range of basic programs that Quebec universities must offer, notably at the under-graduate level. Or it may extend into graduate school programs already in existence in the university. Other programs will complement areas of special-ization previously developed by the university.

The new program must ensure its viability over a period of at least five years by recruiting sufficient students. Finally, it is essential that the university has or can secure adequate financial resources. At the very heart of the evalu-ation of timeliness is an assessment of the budgetary impact of a project, not only the exact amount needed to set up the program, but also the annual development needs.

Quality Assurance and Existing Programs

The universities themselves are also responsible for assuring the quality of their *existing* programs and have recently introduced, within the framework of CREPUQ, a new review system along the lines of the UK Academic Audit Unit. Towards the end of the 1980s all sorts of factors set the scene for innovation in this area. It was no longer felt that one could simply say that the universities had taken all necessary steps to guarantee the quality of their services. Budgets that tightened every year, the need for increased productiv-ity, economies that became ever more open and competitive, the growing demand for competence and technological capability, in short, the need to do more with less, required policy decisions that were sensitive to both the distribution and use of resources.

In March 1991, to ensure that every university had and applied a program evaluation policy, Quebec universities adopted a *Politique relative à l'évaluation périodique des programmes existants*. Above all, the universities wished to make sure that their policies responded to a body of norms and conditions that were recognized collectively and would satisfy society's demand for quality university education.

To give it substance and credibility, the new system has an external audit function, the execution of which is entrusted to a Commission composed of five members named by CREPUQ's Executive Committee; its mandate is to examine the adequacy of policies and practices in force in Quebec universities as compared to the norms and conditions laid out in CREPUQ's *Politique* and to make recommendations where necessary.

The Commission has complete autonomy in the exercise of its mandate. Its recommendations are sent directly to the university involved and are not subject to any prior approval by CREPUQ. It exercises a strictly moral authority. Some would suggest that this is not sufficient, but the Commission's short history has already confirmed that this decision was a wise one. Its reports are in the public domain and to judge by reaction to its first two reports, the work of the Commission has been well received by the public and already enjoys considerable credibility. There are other clear indications of success: the first university for whom the Commission verified an evaluation procedure made substantial changes to its institutional policy, while a second is preparing to revise policy in light of the Commission's recommendations. Similar steps are being taken in other places in preparation for the next visits by the Commission.

Conclusion

The development of communication technologies and the growing interdependence of markets and national economies have profoundly modified the conditions under which our societies are evolving. These new realities place before the nations of the world challenges to creativity whose breadth and complexity it would have been difficult to imagine fifteen years ago.

In a socio-economic scenario dominated by competitive goals, where the demand for qualified manpower and competence of all kinds is growing every day, the universities will certainly be called upon to play an essential role. Those responsible for training in professional fields and disciplines will want to ensure that the programs they offer and the degrees they grant meet high standards of relevance and quality.

Furthermore, education is funded in large part by the State, at least as regards the public sector. Under these circumstances, it is normal that governments take a close interest in the way educational institutions perform and require that their use of public funds is transparent. What is commonly called accountability is carried out at different levels in different countries, and according to a wide variety of balances and proportions when it comes to division of jurisdictions and institutional responsibilities. Accountability rests on a variety of legislations, institutions and traditions which determine the nature of the links forged between establishments of higher learning and the public authorities. Within their own particular constraints the various units and agencies pursue the common goal of quality.

References

CREPUQ (1988) 'L'évaluation des projets de nouveaux programmes des universités québécoises', November.

CREPUQ (1991) 'Politique des établissements universitaires du Quebec relative à l'évaluation périodique des programmes existants', March.

CREPUQ (1992) 'Protocole de vérification', Commission de vérification de l'évaluation des programmes, April.

CONSEIL DES UNIVERSITÉS (1991) 'L'évaluation des projets de nouveaux programmes', November.

WILLIAMS, P. (1991) 'The CVCP Academic Audit Unit', Birmingham.

Chapter 10

Romania: A Case Study from Central and Eastern Europe

Iulian Beju

Since the dramatic political upheavals of 1989, countries in central and eastern Europe have been struggling to restructure their higher education systems and develop appropriate criteria and procedures for quality assessment and accreditation. Research and development in Romania leading to legislation, draft accreditation standards, and a proposed Commission of Academic Assessment are described.

Since 1989 the criteria and procedures of quality assessment and accreditation of higher education institutions have been widely discussed in Central and Eastern Europe, alongside the need for bilateral recognition of studies, diplomas, and degrees. Some trends and issues have an obvious affinity with the structure and interests of similar institutions in Western Europe. All are operating in a general context of decentralization, computerization and information technology, and the need to diversify financial resources, establish links with industry, and train specialists for the immediate needs of economic and social life. All are dealing with matters relating to the selection and training of teaching and research staff, and the inertia of some, and responding to the particular needs of their own community.

There are differences in types of provision, for example, distance education is not well established in Central and Eastern Europe and traditional continuing education is not efficient; and there are real and valuable differences between countries arising from their specific national cultures and higher education systems. But there are also differences which arise because Europe is still divided into two worlds. Central and Eastern Europe is searching for ways of transition in as painless a way as possible from communist ideology and totalitarian regimes towards market economy and pluralist democracy, while Western Europe is taking important steps towards economic and political integration. For both, this means first destroying old structures and then building up new ones.

An essential characteristic of the transition period for Central and Eastern Europe, with direct consequences for education, is the instability of social, economic and cultural life, of government and of inter-ethnic relationships.

The education system is bound to play an essential part in the restructuring process, for the future depends mainly on the quality of the younger generation. Higher education institutions can assimilate quickly the experience of other countries, and can contribute to the achievement of the necessary changes.

Towards Reform of Higher Education Institutions in Central and Eastern Europe

Following the major reforms of 1989 in the economic, social and political life of ex-communist countries, higher education is now considered a priority by all governments and political parties. Unfortunately, there is generally no long-term educational strategy. As a result, many of the changes are only partial, having mostly a restorative character. The partial changes often trigger others, giving the image of effervescence rather than of systematic reconstruction. Nevertheless three major movements in the horizontal structure of higher education systems can be identified:

- an extension of education as reflected in the growing number of institutions and students;
- a structural diversification of existing institutions through new faculties in fields previously neglected such as ecology, management, business administration, informatics; and
- the creation of private universities: Romania has over forty, and their number is still increasing.

There are also vertical changes. The uniform study period inherited from the communist regime has been replaced by greater diversity at both undergraduate and postgraduate levels. And interest in distance education and open universities is developing.

This rapid and somewhat unpredictable expansion has led to a considerable growth in the demand for human and material resources, not always at hand. As a result, either a general decrease of average academic standards in the whole system, or a strong stratification of higher education institutions arising from the privileged access to resources of some institutions is anticipated.

Beside these structural changes within individual countries, higher education in Central and Eastern Europe is also adjusting to international inter-university cooperation in the framework of the programs launched by the European Community (TEMPUS, ERASMUS, EURISTOTE, and Action Jean Monnet). All these programs lay stress on the mobility of students, staff and researchers, and raise questions about compatibility of studies, criteria and methods of professional assessment. To cope with these new issues, Central and Eastern European countries, as beneficiaries of these programs of cooperation, have independently tried to restructure their higher education systems appropriately. The opportunity for evolution has resulted in two complementary tendencies: the integration (or copying) of efficient systems, and diversification and the creation of new structures. However, the absence of clear and widely accepted academic standards has exercised a negative influence on both public and private higher education institutions. In Romania, the Ministry of Education has decided to follow the international example in introducing accreditation of higher education institutions, and this may become a landmark for the future.

Towards Accreditation in Romania

The Ministry began with a large research study which made an inventory of the main systems of quality assessment and accreditation of higher education institutions in other countries, their methods, procedures and means of implementation. Comparative analysis of their compatibility as well as their common features and characteristics, indicates that:

- a great diversity of procedures despite the strong long-term contacts between these institutions;
- assessment methods and procedures cannot be transferred to another country without adjustment to the local situation;
- internationally, there is urgent interest in quality assessment in higher education: the last ten years have witnessed the establishment of a large number of accreditation bodies, and some traditional procedures have been replaced by new ones;
- countries differ significantly in the extent of government involvement in accreditation;
- each country has a tendency to create its own systems of quality assessment and control, but all have as a common aim the achievement of an acknowledged international standard in the educational process;
- the rapid changes in higher education in some of the Central and Eastern European countries and elsewhere require a dynamic accreditation system; and
- considering the ever-growing mobility of students, staff and researchers, the accreditation system must involve international comparisons.

The accreditation system proposed for Romania is specific to a country with an explosive development of public and private higher education, and it takes into account that Romanian legislation concerning education as a whole is still being elaborated. Following this study, a draft law concerning 'the accreditation procedure in higher education institutions and the national recognition of diplomas' has been submitted to the Romanian Parliament. In this legislation, accreditation applies to all higher education institutions—established universities or institutes, new state institutions, and private institutions. Standards are set by reference to those at some of the traditional universities or institutes, and by comparison with appropriate institutions in other countries. Accreditation proceeds in two stages:

- *initial accreditation*: the issue of a licence for the whole higher education institution, (or for some faculties or departments only) on the basis of minimal criteria concerning educational planning and programs, professional personnel, selection of students, physical and financial resources; and
- *level accreditation*: assessment of the training level of the institution, by comparison with levels elsewhere. Accreditation level is determined by means of tests taken by all students of the institution alongside those from standard institutions; an overlap of 85 per cent in the results leads to level A, overlap of 70–85 per cent results in level B; 55–70 per cent for level C. Below 55 per cent means closure for the institution: this is intended to maintain high standards.

As described by the General Secretary of the Romanian Board for Quality Assurance and Accreditation of Higher Education (Ifrim, 1993), initial accreditation is based on nine standards or criteria, for each of which a score of 1–10 points is allocated:

- *academic integrity*: even where the institution is totally or partially self-financed, it should not operate for profit and should not be used for political purposes;
- *planning*: there should be a well-considered prospective program, setting out objectives, structure, development possibilities, organization, and financing;
- *management*: satisfactory structures and regulations, and provision for student participation are required;
- *educational programs* should be coherent and appropriate in content and delivery;
- *teaching personnel*: there should be an attested, stable staff with an adequate salary structure, contractual arrangements and professional development opportunities;
- *support facilities* such as library, textbooks, laboratories and computers, study space must be adequate;
- *student services and facilities* should support both the intellectual and physical development of the students;
- *physical resources* must be appropriate; and
- *financial resources* should be stable, free from external influence or pressure, and sufficient for the achievement of the stated objectives.

Compliance with the requirements of these standards will be appraised from the institution's self-report and other documentation, staff lists, information about student performance, employment prospects, Board of Accreditation reports, and visits to the institution. The Ministry of Education and Science will do the accreditation through a Commission of Academic Assessment and a body of specialists associated to it. Each year it will publish a list of accredited institutions, specifying the level of accreditation.

Conclusion

The UNESCO International Convention regarding the recognition of studies and degrees draws attention to the need for comparative procedures which are accepted worldwide concerning quality assessment and accreditation in higher education. This case study may be useful for countries within and outside Central and Eastern Europe who are also addressing increased expenditure on higher education, expansion of educational systems and forms, continuous growth in student numbers, and proliferation of academic subjects, as well as considering how higher education can meet the present and future demands of society, international cooperation between institutions, and student, staff and researcher mobility.

Reference

IFRIM, M. (1993) 'Accreditation norms and procedures for the institutions of higher education in Romania', *QA Newsletter*, Hong Kong, 3, January.

Chapter 11

Quality Assessment in Scotland

Jim Donaldson

In 1992 the Scottish Higher Education Funding Council (SHEFC) was established. Its role in assessing the quality of educational provision offered by universities and colleges in Scotland is outlined, together with some comments on the first year of operation. Based on a pilot study, the Council has agreed a method and process of evaluating cognate subject areas, within a detailed Quality Framework (see Annex).

Background

Government regards quality assessment as a central part of its higher education reforms, and the Scottish Higher Education Funding Council (SHEFC) is obliged by the Further and Higher Education (Scotland) Act of 1992 to undertake assessments in universities and colleges and to have regard to the outcome of such assessments when determining funding for institutions.

The Higher Education White Paper, published in 1991, distinguished between quality control, quality audit and quality assessment. Responsibility for *quality control* resides with the higher education institutions themselves: The Higher Education Quality Council (HEQC) has responsibility for *quality audit*, providing external scrutiny comparable with that provided previously in the polytechnic and college sector by the Council for National Academic Awards (CNAA) and, more recently in the university sector, by the Academic Audit Unit (AAU) of the Committee of Vice-Chancellors and Principals. The HEQC has a UK-wide remit to audit institutions' internal procedures for defining, maintaining and enhancing quality, with the purpose of assuring clients (students, employers, Funding Councils and government) that systems are in place and operate effectively. The Funding Councils in England, Scotland and Wales each operate their own arrangements for *quality assessment*. Those for Scotland are described here; the other Councils have a broadly similar approach, but there are some differences in practice and experience. (For an account of the early work of the English Funding Council, see Thomas, 1993).

SHEFC responsibility for external evaluation of the actual provision of education — of the quality of teaching and learning — involves subject-specific assessment by peer scrutiny of institutional documentation and student work,

direct observation of teaching, interviews, and reference to performance indicators such as cost per student, and attainment, completion and employment
rates. Assessment of research quality is undertaken separately. The general
purposes are:

- to provide a basis for advice on the quality of educational provision in
  institutions funded by the Council;
- to produce reports which identify strengths and weaknesses, promote
  good practice and stimulate improvement;
- to monitor trends in the quality of provision relative to resources and
  the implementation of recommendations in earlier reports; and encourage progressive improvement by a programme of revisiting;
- to provide a basis for advice to the Council on the promotion and
  maintenance of quality through innovations and developments in
  curriculum, teaching and assessment; and
- to inform students and employers on the quality of provision, thereby
  promoting competition and choice.

Before arriving at an agreed procedure the Secretary of State for Education and Science commissioned a series of pilot projects to develop and evaluate
a method of assessing the quality of teaching and learning in specific areas
within institutions, and of reporting to the Funding Councils on the quality
of work across institutions in order to inform funding decisions. The focus
of the pilot assessments was on the methods to be used rather than on the
judgments on quality in the four volunteer institutions. There were therefore
no published reports, but the key issues were reflected in discussion documents and consultation papers circulated to all higher education institutions in
Scotland. Institutions gave a clear expression of their views and the SHEFC
modified its assessment method to incorporate most of their suggested
amendments.

Quality Defined

'Quality' does not lend itself to easy or precise definition, but there is general
agreement that the quality of any activity should be assessed in relation to its
purpose. For that reason, the SHEFC quality assessment is conducted in the
context of an institution's own declared aims, purposes and mission using a
'quality framework' which identifies eleven 'aspects' of provision as set out in
the Annex.

'Aims and Curricula' are the first focus of the Framework; assessment of
provision is set in the context of institutional mission and aims, department
or faculty aims and, more specifically, course aims and objectives. 'Curriculum Design' is expected to reflect and serve these aims. 'The Teaching and
Learning Environment', and 'Staff Resources and Learning Resources' are

essentially 'inputs' to the teaching and learning process, but contribute to the overall quality assessment as proxies for more direct assessment of the processes themselves or their outcomes. 'Course Organisation', 'Teaching and Learning Practice', 'Student Support', and 'Assessment and Monitoring' may all be viewed as aspects of the 'delivery' process but are separated for ease of understanding. 'Student Work' is the most visible and immediate evidence of outcomes of the learning process and is of interest to quality assessors not as an indication of the academic standards prevailing in the subject, which is properly a matter for external examiners, but as an indication of the quality of the teaching, learning and assessment processes. (External examiners in the UK are usually senior academics who visit departments broadly similar to their own in two or three other institutions. They read a sample of examination scripts, and discuss with staff the coverage of the examination paper and the marking schedule. Their primary purpose is to ensure comparability of standards among institutions in the award of degree courses). In looking at 'Quality Control', assessors are less interested in the institutional quality systems and processes, which is the concern of the HEQC Division of Quality Audit, than in how well such arrangements actually work in the cognate area being assessed.

Many would argue that quality is best assessed by direct comparison of results with intentions. However, this is difficult in practice. Results which are measured by, for example, graduate output and post-course destinations do not of themselves provide a basis for definitive assessments of quality and they are in any case available only after a considerable time has elapsed. Outcomes of higher education such as values and scholarship do not lend themselves to precise assessment. Nevertheless, the use of such performance indicators (PIs) is one important part of the process.

The Assessment Method

The SHEFC's quality assessment method is founded on 'self-assessment' by institutions. This recognizes both the diversity of missions and approaches to quality assurance in institutions and also the wealth of expertise built up by the AAU and the CNAA and within the institutions themselves.

Both the self-assessment and the subsequent external assessment process use the Quality Framework as an operational device which will be progressively refined from year to year. While the eleven 'aspects' of the Framework represent the major dimensions of the quality of educational provision as defined by the Council, it is not intended that each one should be slavishly applied in all contexts. The assessment is carried out by practitioners in that subject area, seconded from higher education institutions throughout the UK, and by assessors drawn from industry and commerce. They are supported by staff in the Council's Quality Assessment Directorate, all of whom have a background of teaching in higher education.

Assessment is conducted on the basis of 'cognate areas', that is distinct homogeneous subject-areas such as economics, electrical and electronic engineering, chemistry, history, etc. within broad subject groups. All institutions offering a substantial level of provision in a particular cognate area are included in the self-assessment stage of the process but thereafter a degree of sampling is applied. Not all institutions will necessarily be visited and, in those visited, only a representative sample of provision — arrived at by consultation between assessors and the institution — will be assessed. In 1993–4 assessments were made against a four-point scale, namely: excellent, highly satisfactory, satisfactory or unsatisfactory.

The Assessment Process

Institutions are advised of the cognate areas to be assessed in March to allow them to carry out self-assessments by the end of June. These self-assessments are then scrutinized by specialist Lead Assessors drawn from higher education institutions and coordinated by Council staff. Decisions are taken about the sample of institutions to be visited, including all those claiming to be 'excellent' in that area, as well as a selection of others. Institutions are notified of visits in early September and arrangements made for 'pre-visits' as necessary to finalize administrative arrangements.

The main assessment visit normally occupies two or three days within one working week, during which a team of three to five assessors meets students and staff, views facilities and observes teaching and learning. All documentary information submitted to SHEFC will have been studied before the visit. At the end of the visit, there is a meeting with representatives of the institution to ensure that assessors have all the evidence they need. A draft written report is discussed with senior management in the institution to provide a final check on matters of factual accuracy, and to give feedback on the findings of the assessment team (although this feedback stops short of an overall summative assessment). The Council's Quality Assessment Committee then receives and considers the report and makes recommendations to Council on publication. Published reports summarize the main assessment findings which are made available not only to the institution but also more generally.

Assessment in Practice

During 1992–3 economics and electrical engineering were assessed. In their self-assessments, ten providers in Scotland claimed excellence in the former, seven in the latter. Reports from the assessment panels deemed economics in four institutions and electrical engineering in three to be excellent; the 'prizes' were an extra 5 per cent of funded places. Another eighty reports are expected during 1994.

Writing from the perspective of one Scottish institution, Reid (1993) comments that reaction to the quality assessment exercise has been rather more positive in Scotland than in England. He suggests this may derive from its much smaller number of institutions which engenders a closer education and academic community and more opportunities for consultation between officials and academics. The SHEFC can visit every institution offering studies in a particular area within a year, whereas in England only sampling is possible.

> This distances the central body, weakens the arguments in favour of peer evaluation carried out in open discussion, reinforces the impor- tance of written criteria for the assessment and undermines any overall views stated by the Quality Assessment Committee about the health of any particular subject area in the country. As a consequence, the first year of operation in Scotland has been received remarkably well. Such reservations as have been raised relate to:
>
> - the potential for inconsistency across different cognate areas given the imprecise statements of criteria; and within cognate areas given the changes of personnel;
> - notwithstanding claims that the assessment was based on the in- stitutions' own stated aims, evidence of implicit aims about the nature of higher education expected by the panel;
> - the cost of the exercise;
> - the boundaries of cognate areas; and
> - the duplication caused by each visit to a particular institution wishing to see the student support facilities, e.g. library, careers. (Reid, 1993)

Conclusion

After its first year of operation, the SHEFC invited an independent evaluation of its approach. In concluding that the SHEFC has made a promising start in its quality assessment, the evaluator's report (Barnett, 1993) makes a number of recommendations about the purpose and use of the Quality Framework, the conduct of the visits, the choice of assessors, feedback to the institutions, and the nature of the published reports. The report comments on the link between funding and assessment, wondering whether resources might be used to assist rather than penalize institutions/departments with 'unsatisfactory' judgments and whether the rewards for a good teaching-quality assessment are worth the effort being invested, and observes:

> If institutions conclude that the opportunity costs are too severe, the potential of the quality assessments for improving quality is likely to be severely diminished. This raised a fundamental question about the

underlying purpose of the exercise: is it intended generally to improve the overall quality of the system or is it intended primarily to ensure that standards do not fall below an acceptable threshold? (Barnett, 1993).

The SHEFC anticipates that the process of quality assessment, and the respective roles of institutions, assessors and SHEFC staff will continue to evolve. Possibilities of collaboration and harmonization with the HEQC, accrediting bodies and the institutions themselves are being explored and the approach outlined here will be adapted and developed. Ultimately, quality assurance and enhancement should be a cooperative exercise by all concerned.

References

BARNETT, R. (1993) *SHEFC Quality Assessment: an evaluation*, SHEFC.

DEPARTMENT OF EDUCATION AND SCIENCE (1991) *Higher Education: a New Framework*, Cmnd. 1541, London, HMSO.

REID, A. (1993) 'Quality assurance in higher education' internal document, Queen Margaret College, Scotland.

SCHULLER, T. (Ed) (1991) *The Future of Higher Education*, Guildford, SRHE/Open University Press.

THOMAS, A. (1993) 'Performance Funding', INQAAHE Conference, Montreal.

WARREN, J. (1992) 'Learning as an indicator of educational Quality', *Studies in Higher Education*, 17, pp. 337–47.

Annex: Quality Framework

Aims and Curricula

- Curriculum aims and objectives are explicit and known to staff and students.
- Specialist aims and objectives are consistent with institutional mission and aims.
- Aims and objectives correspond to the needs of students, society and the economy, as revealed by systematic investigation.
- Curricula accurately reflect declared aims and objectives and the needs identified.
- Curricula provide an appropriate balance of specialist content, general conceptual skills and personal, transferable skills.
- Curricula are up-to-date in terms of specialist developments and current thinking on curriculum development and delivery.

Curriculum Design and Review

[By 'course' is meant any coherent learning programme which may be evaluated in its own right.]

- Courses are imaginatively designed to meet as effectively as possible the needs of the full range of intended students, in terms of course length/duration, modes of attendance, location, structure and sequence, optional elements etc.
- Appropriate provision is made for alternative curricular modes such as accreditation of prior learning (APL), credit accumulation and transfer (CAT), work-based learning (WBL), open learning (OL), distance learning (DL) etc.
- Course design seeks to maximize access for: students with special needs, disadvantaged groups, applicants with non-standard qualifications, mature entrants etc.
- Courses are periodically reviewed to assess their suitability and adjustments made within a reasonable timescale.
- There is regular liaison between the institution and industry, commerce, public agencies, professional bodies and other potential end-users.

The Teaching and Learning Environment

- The academic environment, physical and social, is generally conducive to learning, and the level of research and other scholarly activities is appropriate to the level of teaching.
- Teaching accommodation is sufficient in quantity and appropriate for the curriculum on offer and for the full range of students.
- There are adequate specialist facilities — including practical and experiential learning facilities — for the curriculum on offer.
- Ancillary facilities — staff accommodation, storage space, preparation rooms, amenity accommodation etc. — are adequate.
- The physical environment is well maintained in terms of decor, cleanliness, repairs, safety and necessary modifications.
- Accommodation, especially specialist accommodation, is effectively deployed and imaginatively used: as evidenced by suitable plans, schedules, timetables and control systems.

Staff Resources

- The teaching-staff establishment is sufficient to deliver the curriculum.
- The teaching-staff complement is suitable for the curriculum, in terms of the mix of qualifications, experience, aptitudes, age, status etc.
- There is adequate support in terms of library, technician, administrative, student services, staffing, etc.
- Staff resources are effectively deployed: roles and relationships are well-defined and understood; duties allocated appropriate to qualifications, experience and aptitude; there is provision for review, consultation and redeployment.
- Staff-development needs are systematically identified, in relation to individual aspirations, the curriculum and institutional requirements.
- All staff, academic and support, regularly undertake appropriate staff development related to identified needs: induction, in-service training, secondments, consultancy, research and other scholarly activities.

Learning Resources

- There are sufficient physical resources to deliver the curriculum, including equipment, materials and information technology.
- Equipment is up-to-date, readily available and effectively deployed.
- Library, audio-visual, computer and other academic services are adequate for the curriculum.

Course Organization

- Learning programmes ('courses') are effectively organized and managed.
- Teaching programmes are clearly articulated, made known to students and regularly monitored.
- Coursework and assessment are systematically scheduled and coordinated among lecturers and specialisms.
- Feedback is regularly obtained from students, employers, moderators and auditors, and analysed and acted upon as appropriate.

Teaching and Learning Practice

- Teaching and learning are based on explicit objectives which are consistent with course aims.
- Teaching methods are innovative, varied, appropriate to the stated objectives and make effective use of available facilities, equipment, materials and aids.
- Teaching is well planned and prepared and effectively performed, taking account of the needs of all categories of student.
- The pace of teaching and learning takes due account of the nature of the curriculum, students' varied abilities and prior learning, and the specific needs of the very able and weak students.
- Teaching approaches encourage independent learning and students take responsibility for their own learning.
- Learning is enriched by appropriate reference to cross-curricular links, current research, industrial applications and development of generic skills such as communication and teamwork.

Student Support

- The need of all students for guidance and support is recognized and provision made for advice and assistance in the curricular, vocational and personal domains.
- Responsibility for particular aspects of student support is clearly located and effective liaison maintained between arrangements at course/department level and institution-wide services.
- Adequate provision is made for information and advice to potential students during the application and enrolment phases.

- Students are effectively supported during their studies by systems of induction, course tutors, personal tutors and provision for remediation and curricular choice.
- Students are prepared for the next stage of study or employment by appropriate contacts, information, advice and training.
- Among individual staff there is a general attitude of concern for the well-being of students.

Assessment and Monitoring

- Assessment arrangements correspond to all the aims and aspects of the curriculum as taught.
- A range of assessment methods is used in a planned manner to serve diagnostic, formative and summative purposes.
- The scope and weighting of assessment schemes are clear and known to all concerned and the standards applied are explicit and consistent across the curriculum.
- Procedures are regularly applied to ensure that, as far as possible, assessment schemes are valid, reliable and fairly administered.
- Student progress is systematically recorded and monitored, fed back to students and corrective action taken where necessary.
- Students have ready access to reasonable appeal procedures.

Students' Work

- Coursework is regularly set and assessed and is at the appropriate level of attainment.
- Coursework faithfully reflects the full range of curricular aims, including the development of generic skills.
- Student achievement, as represented by their coursework, is comparable with that of students on similar courses elsewhere.
- Students' performance and attitudes indicate a positive and successful learning experience.

Output, Outcomes and Quality Control

- Performance Indicators are regularly used to inform institutional assessment of achievement in relation to educational aims and objectives.
- Results are monitored and analysed and appropriate action taken.
- Results against these or other appropriate indicators compare favourably with institutional or national norms.
- Quality Control arrangements at institutional, department, subject and/or course level are consistent and coherent.

- Quality standards, policies and strategies, are consistently applied and periodically reviewed within the cognate area.
- There is a general commitment to excellence in teaching and learning, apparent in staff and student attitudes in all aspects of provision.

Chapter 12

Accrediting Vocational Higher Education in South Africa

Danie Jacobs

The educational provision and accreditation arrangements in South Africa's universities, technikons, colleges of education, private colleges, colleges of agriculture, colleges of nursing and Industry Training Boards are all briefly described. Current proposals for a national, vocational qualifications' structure are outlined and the consequent benefits for credit transfer and student mobility noted.

South Africa includes the Republic of South Africa (RSA), and the self-governing territories of Transkei, Bophuthatswana, Venda and Ciskei (the TBVC states). Educational policy is decided by the Minister and Department of National Education; educational provision is the responsibility of sixteen local departments of education, but education or training is also provided by other institutions that are established or administered by the Departments of Manpower, Agriculture, Post and Telecommunications and others. Additionally, the private sector plays a major role through private colleges and in-house training by employers, promoted by levy and grant schemes and administered by Industry Training Boards.

Accreditation and external quality assurance by peer-group evaluation are very recent phenomena in some certain sectors and non-existent in others. With a view to the future, higher education in South Africa needs to include all sectors, with optimal consolidation and rationalization.

The Higher and Vocational Education System

Universities, technikons, colleges of education, technical colleges, private colleges, colleges of agriculture, colleges of nursing and Industry Training Boards, all offer post-school education.

South Africa has eighteen universities. In 1991 there were 308,172 enrolled students of whom 157,432 were Whites, 21,035 Indians, 19,575 Coloureds and 110,130 Blacks. About one-sixth were postgraduates and there were slightly more males than females; nearly 40 per cent were studying by distance education at the University of South Africa. Quality assurance mainly relies on the external examiner system, although there are some recent proposals for a broader quality assurance system under the auspices of the Committee of University Principals (Strydom and Khotseng, 1993).

There are fifteen technikons (polytechnic-type institutions offering higher education, but not degree-granting) which present national programmes on six levels beyond the twelfth school grade. In 1991 there were 104,652 technikon students, three-quarters male. There were 64,735 Whites, 6,743 Indians, 8,946 Coloureds and 24,228 Blacks. Some 12,000 students qualify annually for certificates or diplomas. All curricula are coordinated and approved by the Minister of National Education. Since 1988, the technikons have had authority to conduct internal examinations at all levels but the authority to grant certificates or diplomas rests with the Certification Council for Technikon Education (SERTEC).

Teachers are mainly trained either by universities or by colleges of education. The latter are administered directly by the different Departments of Education, although a recent development is the establishment of college boards giving somewhat greater autonomy. Some colleges have agreements with universities whereby they cooperate in the tuition of students towards university degrees. Apart from these agreements, there is no accreditation system for this sector.

In 1991, the 129 technical colleges had 76,435 students: 50,907 Whites, 5,327 Indians, 5,711 Coloureds and 14,490 Blacks. The programmes offered are for artisan training, secretarial and other commercial fields of study, and the arts. Programme levels range from N1 to N6, with N4, N5 and N6 falling within the higher education sector: however, the full spectrum is currently part of the secondary school administration, with certificates awarded by the South African Certification Council (SAFCERT). The possibility of transferring accreditation of the N4 to N6 components to SERTEC is under consideration. Greater cooperation between technikons and technical colleges is also proposed so that more students taking lower-level technikon programmes can be accommodated in technical colleges. This would ease the pressure on the technikons, where in 1992 approximately 30,000 students were not accepted even though they fulfilled the entrance requirements, because financial resources limited intake numbers.

Private colleges are not subsidized by the State, and there is no system for state approval or recognition of their programmes. Recognition for employment purposes of qualifications awarded rests entirely with the private sector employers, and some are now demanding that private college programmes be accredited by an external authority. There are currently more than 60,000 students enrolled in tertiary education programmes in these colleges; in 1991 an Association of Private Colleges was established with sixty members and the Association is currently investigating college accreditation by SERTEC. To meet employers' demands, the Department of Manpower in 1992 established the National Council for Vocational Training Standards (NCVTS), but this concentrates largely on business and secretarial studies. A system of accreditation for all the programmes in private colleges would not only facilitate recognition by employers, but would hopefully also lead to transfer of credits attained to public sector institutions such as the technikons and technical colleges.

Established and financed by the Departments of Agriculture, the twelve colleges of agriculture are mainly for training farmers, with a pass in twelfth grade as the entrance requirement. In the self-governing territories, the emphasis has moved recently towards the training of extension officers to advise farmers in those areas. These colleges now have an Association of Principals of Colleges of Agriculture, and are seeking accreditation for the purpose of recognition of their two or three-year diplomas, and to facilitate the possibility of further study in other institutions by diplomates. They are being advised to seek such accreditation or to enter into agreements with those technikons which offer agriculture courses for technicians employed by the Department of Agriculture.

In 1990 there were 9,700 students in the thirty colleges of nursing (in addition to the 1,640 students studying nursing at university). There is a four-year basic nursing qualification and nine post-basic qualifications comprising fifty instructional offerings. The future position of the colleges of nursing within an overall accreditation system is as yet unclear.

There are currently nineteen active Industry Training Boards (ITBs). Some of these have an interest in tertiary education programmes offered at technikons, technical colleges and private colleges. They are invited to participate in technikon accreditation where applicable, and SERTEC assists the ITBs (on request) regarding the handling of standards and accreditation of their member training establishments.

There is also an enormous amount of in-service training taking place in commerce and industry and in the public sector, in many cases with excellent facilities and provision. Much of this, however, is not recognized outside the particular company or organization providing it.

The Need for a National Qualification Structure

The mutual recognition of qualifications or of credits earned in partly completed qualifications at all the above institutions requires urgent attention in the interests of the economy. South Africa has a shortage of trained personnel, with only one high-level trained person for every eighty-five of the economically active population, compared to one in thirteen in the USA. There is a need to make higher education, in whatever form, available to more potential candidates and to facilitate better cooperation between the different providers.

Vocational qualifications based on academic study are well developed in technikons, technical colleges, colleges of nursing, colleges of agriculture and to some extent in private colleges, but in isolated compartments. The development of a national vocational qualification structure to accommodate the systematic comparison of levels and standards of qualifications attained in the different types of institutions, is of the utmost importance. This would facilitate the recognition of credits and qualifications between institutions. It should be possible for students who start their studies in an N1 programme in a technical college, to continue through that college, or to switch to a private college and on to a technikon or university, if they have the capability.

Discussion about the establishment of such a national vocational qualification structure is currently taking place. This would be grouped firstly into smaller sub-units of academic qualifications at primary and secondary, at post-secondary undergraduate, and at postgraduate levels. Secondly, it would be grouped into sub-units of non-academic qualifications based on work competency or proficiency as measured in the workplace, with no relevance to academic qualifications, but with the possibility of partial recognition in formal education programmes. The position of a qualification in the national structure would be the result of regular, compulsory accreditation by a statutory and widely accepted body. Comparison of qualifications would not be attempted by common examinations, but would be on the basis of peer and interest-group evaluation.

Accreditation in Vocational Higher Education

South African universities are self-accrediting, but for vocational higher education a number of external accreditation mechanisms and accreditation bodies, all of very recent origin, do exist.

The Association of Accredited Education Centers of South Africa (ACESA) was established by private sector training institutions and colleges in 1989. Its declared objectives are to lay down minimum standards for educational programmes and to evaluate and accredit them; to promote the participation and involvement of organized industry and commerce in accreditation; and to liaise with other accreditation or certification bodies, industry training boards, government agencies and departments and with the general public. It is a private initiative to encourage cooperation between interested institutions in the private sector towards the improvement and maintenance of educational standards.

The Association of Private Colleges of Southern Africa (APCSA) was established in 1991. College programmes do not require approval by the education authorities and they receive no subsidy from the State. It is a not-for-profit association which aims:

- to foster the highest standard of tuition and training at tertiary level;
- to promote beneficial communication between all private tertiary colleges;
- to represent the interests of members to government, the media employer organizations and the public; and

- to determine and promote acceptable standards of practice and to require adherence, by the members of the Association, to a code of ethics.

As already mentioned, the National Council for Vocational Training Standards (NCVTS) was established in 1992. Its function is to accredit private colleges in terms of their education and training standards, and it currently concentrates mainly on business and secretarial studies.

The Industry Training Boards (ITBs) function to some extent as accreditation bodies of employers that provide training to their employees. They promote training through a levy and grant system. Their experience indicates that a self-imposed evaluation of standards is very effective, and the observance of the strict rules the employers impose on themselves through their ITBs is very encouraging.

A number of professional bodies, e.g., the Medical and Dental Council and its subsidiary bodies in the paramedical fields, the Engineering Council and others, impose standards on educational institutions that must be complied with for professional registration. They have legal authority to discredit educational institutions, by not recognizing qualifications that are below standard. All the professional bodies have accepted invitations to coordinate their evaluation exercises with those of the Certification Council for Technikon Education, whenever the programmes offered by technikons are evaluated.

The Certification Council for Technikon Education (SERTEC) was established in 1986 as a statutory body to monitor the standards of education and examinations in technikons. SERTEC follows an internationally accepted accreditation model. Evaluation is done by visiting committees composed of representatives of professional bodies, employers, educators from other technikons or from universities, and of the SERTEC Council. Visits to technikons commenced in 1991 and are repeated for a different set of programmes every semester. The more than 400 programmes are being scrutinized in the four-year period 1991 to 1994 and repeated thereafter every four years. Accreditation is compulsory and not permanent. It has been well received by the technikons and the employers and professional bodies, and has had a positive effect on the technikons in terms of the raising of educational standards.

Consolidation

Recognition by the institutions of each other's qualifications or credits on a voluntary basis does not take place on the scale necessary for the advancement of human resources in the changing South Africa. At national level, accreditation is seen as an instrument which can assist this process. If undertaken in terms of the anticipated vocational qualification structure, it would allow qualifications attained at any accredited educational institution to be classified into a specific level of the structure and recognized elsewhere. This would facilitate student mobility and avoid duplication of programmes. International recognition of qualifications or credits is a logical next step, and ideally should include vocational as well as academic higher education provision.

Reference

STRYDOM, A.H. and KHOTSENG, B.M. (1993) 'The Transformation of Universities in South Africa and Approaches to Quality Assurance', Paper presented at the INQAAHE Conference, Montreal, Canada.

Chapter 13

Changing Emphases in the USA

Steven Crow

Written by the Deputy Director of one of the six large regional accrediting agencies in the United States, this chapter explains the background to the federal government's challenge to America's long-established system of higher education quality assurance through voluntary self-regulation. He then outlines how accrediting agencies are responding to current criticisms.

The American experiment in voluntary self-regulation of higher education is entering a new phase that might well spell its demise. For almost a hundred years educators in the United States, through a rich variety of accrediting associations, have accepted the responsibilities both to define the attributes of quality higher education and to measure institutions of higher education against them. Those defining attributes — whether called standards, criteria, or characteristics — have changed over time. So, also, have the processes by which institutions were measured. But it was educators themselves, supported at best by very small professional staffs, who did this important work. This new phase does not result from the desire of educators to step away from these responsibilities; instead, it is shaped by a variety of forces, the understanding of which is essential to anyone considering voluntary self-regulation as a viable means of maintaining quality and order in higher education anywhere.

The author's own organization, the North Central Association of Colleges and Schools began to accredit institutions of higher education in 1913. For many decades, the accrediting activity was largely a paper process. Applying institutions were measured against quantifiable standards on such matters as size of library collection, size of endowment, number and credentials of faculty, and so forth. Site visits, especially for applying or troubled institutions, complemented the process until the early 1960s when mandatory on-site visits became the central activity around which accrediting decisions were made.

The use of quantifiable standards changed, too. They remain an important part of almost all accrediting activities. However, starting in the 1930s, accrediting associations have striven to build into their quantifiable standards the flexibility necessary to allow for the acceptance and support of diverse types and missions of institutions of higher education in the United States.

Over the last decade in particular, most accrediting associations have changed rather dramatically the emphasis they place on things that can be counted. For example, library volumes might still be counted, but library usage and library access to electronic databases are equally important. Faculty numbers and credentials are still calculated, but measures of student achievement figure prominently in the calculus of accreditation. Some suggest that in reaching their decisions today accreditors today measure 'outcomes' — institutional achievements and accomplishments — more carefully than they measure 'inputs' — institutional resources and structures.

In the United States accreditors are now being told that institutional accreditation no longer has any proven value either to institutions or to the public at large. Some people both within and without academia have concluded that accreditation is a process that has outlived its usefulness, and anyone contemplating the implementation of an accreditation program should understand some of the current challenges.

The Changing Scene

Rising Expectations

Higher education in the United States is expected to fulfill a great variety of needs. Not only is it to educate the leaders and professionals of our society, it also is to train the workforce for today and the future, to support the basic research for scientific and technological growth, to serve as a laboratory and a catalyst for creative pluralism in American society, and to find solutions to various social, economic, racial, and political problems within the nation. Moreover, within a changing global context, it is supposed to position the nation to maintain ascendancy in the world order of things.

Where higher education used to focus almost entirely on young students fresh from high school, it now tries to meet the educational needs of every adult citizen. The fact is, the higher education system in the United States has done remarkable jobs both of meeting those expectations and justifying their ever-increasing expansion. But not all promises can be delivered as quickly and as effectively as people want. When higher education fails to meet all of the expectations that it encourages, its support wanes. Right now, the perceived failings of higher education — actually, education in general — seem to be receiving exceptional attention; some of the critics say that accreditors share the responsibility for these failings.

Straitened Financial Times

It is no longer clear how much Americans are willing to pay for quality higher education. Today significant moneys pour from the federal coffers into higher education through student financial-aid programs, programs of funded research, and special allocations sponsored by legislators in Washington, D.C. As the nation searches for places to control its costs, the unexpected costs of student financial aid have become one focus of attention. In the 1980s, the fateful decision was made to finance a significant portion of US higher education by putting students into debt. While the politics — even the ideological underpinnings — of federal student financial aid might be high-minded and democratic, the reality bitterly disappoints many. Years after the money was spent, the public has come to understand the extent of its unexpected investment, and it resents the surprise. Multi-million dollar student-default statistics appear to receive greater attention than do multi-million dollar airplanes that do not fly very well. Even though most of the defaults are concentrated in a specific type of institution, all of higher education has suffered. It must be ineffective education, the cry goes, that has led to student loan defaults. Institutions of higher education clearly have failed too many students. Even worse, the groups responsible for attesting to educational effectiveness — the accreditors — are assumed to have allowed this to happen.

Over-built Systems

Historians may ultimately conclude that US higher education became over-built in the 1960–70s. Not only were large numbers of institutions constructed to serve the baby-boomers, but new types of institutions were started to open higher education to all segments of American society. We are no longer sure we can support financially this massive array of institutions. As other components of state and federal financing become prominent (health care is currently the most significant), public-education budgets have come under more and more scrutiny. Many states show good faith in trying to protect the finances of higher education, but many have cut those funds, or the growth of those funds. In defending the cuts and dwindling support, people point to the perceived ineffectiveness of higher education. If accreditors are useless in closing institutions, they are of no help in solving this unique situation.

The Cultural Quagmire

During the 1980s a strident political note entered the discussion, a note sounded most consistently and most stridently by those who attacked higher education. They claimed that liberals controlled the higher education establishment and pushed leftist ideological viewpoints onto students while denigrating the importance of western civilization. The struggles over the content of the curriculum quickly drew attention to educators who were portrayed as doctrinaire and spoiled inhabitants of the ivory towers of US colleges and universities. No one cares about real teaching, just about doing research on arcane matters or, even worse, on matters smacking of multiculturalism and polysexism. As groups from the left and right fight over who gets to hold it, the torch of intellectual freedom and intellectual objectivity has come perilously close to being dropped. Higher education gets a bad name. Accreditors got caught in this struggle in the early 1990s; they were damaged because of it.

The Governmental Agenda

Although the federal government claims that its involvement in higher education is minimal because, constitutionally, states are responsible for education, the fact is that it has significant influence through its programs that fund students and research. In fact, many will argue that the higher education community has become so dependent on federal largess that it has willingly acquiesced to governmental influence. From scientific research funded by the Department of Defense, NASA, or National Institutes of Health through theatre and arts programming supported by the National Endowment for the Arts or the National Endowment for the Humanities, the federal government is a big player in higher education. The change in administrations perhaps changes some of the priorities of the federal agenda, but there remains a powerful agenda nonetheless.

Obviously, by agreeing to serve the quasi-governmental role of gate-keepers for institutional access to federal student funds, regional institutional accrediting associations have step-by-step initiated a delicate dance of dependency with the federal government, a dance of apparently willing but non-complementary partners. Now, through the 1992 revision of the Higher Education Reauthorization Act and the subsequent recognition requirements proposed by the Secretary of Education, the federal partner has made a bold move to shape the accrediting process to assure that accreditation furthers the federal agenda.

Regionalism

Through the accident of history, institutional accreditation became highly regional in character. In light of the national agenda and in the face of technological changes that free education from the campus, putting it on national computer networks and cable television, the regional approach is rapidly becoming antiquated. Yet each regional organization has its own structures, approaches, and organizational strength that make stronger national approaches difficult. Because institutional accreditors speak with many voices instead of one, the sceptics conclude that accreditation is ineffective at best.

The Concept of Self-regulation

Associations for self-regulation reflected perfectly the nineteenth-century American political culture that held that centralized power was to be feared.

The reasoning was that educators, not politicians and bureaucrats, were best equipped to evaluate the quality of higher education and to protect the integrity of higher education from undue influence of politicians, religious leaders, and so forth. Today that reasoning is no longer accepted as valid, either by the public or by public policy makers. Those most anxious to change radically the accrediting practices in the US, decry the efficacy of peer review. Professions have become self-protective, lawyers protecting bad lawyers, doctors protecting bad doctors, and educators protecting bad and ineffective educators and educational institutions. As private membership associations, accrediting agencies are secretive, holding almost everything as confidential, and more interested in covering for the weak and ineffectual institution than in holding it up to public view. In short, the nineteenth-century American answer to the question of regulation of public services will no longer serve the twenty-first century.

So, from almost every corner higher education has come under attack both from within and without, and many have concluded that voluntary self-regulation is at best incompetent and at worst too self-serving to be a trustworthy tool. Institutional accreditors have been surprised by the strength of these attacks and have had real difficulty in mounting a unified, convincing defence of voluntary accreditation.

Responses

Accrediting agencies have responded to some of these critiques in the following ways:

Revising and Strengthening Standards

With very few exceptions, institutional accrediting agencies have undertaken a major revision of their accrediting standards and processes. Through these revisions, they hope to regain the confidence of some, if not all, of their critics.

Re-emphasizing the Centrality of Teaching and Learning

Several of the new assessment initiatives, although perhaps initiated by federal and state demands for accountability, are addressing the basic culture of higher education. Certainly, the North Central Association of College and Schools believes it has had an impact on its institutions and on the public, through its demand that accreditation focus on the proven effectiveness of teaching and learning.

Rethinking Public Disclosure

Aware that the clubby atmosphere of accreditation must change, many institutional agencies are searching for ways to communicate with the public more clearly and accurately.

Finding New and Better Ways to Tell the Story of Accreditation

Some associations are conducting research to document if and how accreditation is effective. Some are coordinating public relations programs. In short, the view is that accreditation is getting an unfair press, and accreditors must be more aggressive in presenting the real story.

Regrouping and Restructuring

The demise of the Council on Postsecondary Accreditation (COPA) results from many things, but among them was the view held by some within the accrediting community that as a national umbrella organization, COPA was not effective. What takes COPA's place will be of considerable interest, particularly if the regional associations take this opportunity to turn to national cooperative programs through a new national organization.

Conclusion

One thing is clear, institutional accrediting associations must change if they wish to continue to share with federal and state agencies in defining what constitutes quality in higher education. The struggle, then, is not over change. It is, instead, over the nature of that change. Regional accrediting associations have proven their capacity to adapt to new challenges without forfeiting their own well-considered definitions of educational and institutional quality, definitions that emerge from the educational community rather than from legislative bodies or governmental agencies. If they abdicate the rights of members to make and enforce those definitions, they will become little more than compliance arms of the Department of Education or servants of state bureaucracies. However, to survive they must acknowledge the pitfalls of regionalism, the need to assist institutions in adjusting to changed and ever-changing educational agendas, and their responsibility for strengthening the reliability of systems of peer review.

Part 3

International Aspects

Chapter 14

International Linkages and Quality Assurance: A Shifting Paradigm

Marjorie Peace Lenn

The demand for international quality assurance comes from outside and from within higher education. External sources of pressure include professional bodies, regional trade agreements, international higher education associations and global assistance organizations. Internal pressures derive from the expanding export trade in higher education systems, institutions and programs. This chapter reviews some existing and developing international linkages, with particular reference to North America.

The Context of International Quality Assurance

The decade of the 1990s has begun and will likely conclude with quality as a major theme. In industry, commerce, government and now higher education, a focus on quality abounds. Its assessment and enhancement, and attempts to define and measure it, are major issues for higher education throughout the world, not only because of the growing demand within countries for better higher education with fewer resources, but also because of the growing interdependence of national higher education systems. The accelerating international mobility of students, scholars and professionals has motivated educators throughout the world to assure the quality of their products in pursuit of mutual recognition. Where processes of determining educational quality have been non-existent, new ones are being developed. Where they have been in place for some time, the globalization of higher education is influencing their purpose and practice.

This chapter uses the definition of quality assurance offered by the International Network of Quality Assurance Agencies in Higher Education:

quality assurance may relate to a programme, an institution or a whole higher education system. In each case, quality assurance is all of those attitudes, objects, actions, and procedures which, through their existence and use, and together with the quality control activities, ensure that appropriate academic standards are being maintained and enhanced in and by the programme, institution or system, and make this known to the educational community and the public at large (Woodhouse, 1992).

Quality assurance comes in various forms such as accreditation, assessment, academic audit and external examination. Common to each practice is the development of standards; the application of those standards to a program or institution by third parties for the purpose of assessment and enhancement; and the subsequent improvement of the educational entity.

The demand for international quality assurance comes from sources both external and internal to higher education. External pressures include professional bodies, regional trade agreements, international higher education associations and global assistance organizations. Internal pressures include overseas marketing of higher education systems, institutions and programs; stimulated by intrinsic values, global recession, and for some developing countries, a fear of isolation and economic deprivation, educational 'exports' are booming. The educational paradigm is shifting and new models and linkages are challenging us to move beyond the confines of a national perspective toward regional and international issues.

External Pressures for Quality

Professional Bodies

Some professions have formed global organizations and are developing international expectations of quality in professional education. Helsinki in 1992 saw the genesis of international standards for engineering education. And in the same year, when forty-two US specialized accrediting bodies were surveyed, a growing global awareness among the professions and a shift away from traditional national quality assurance arrangements was identified. International activity included:

- *international accreditation*: seventeen out of the forty-two accrediting bodies accredit outside of the United States (fourteen in Canada and five outside of North America), using the accrediting standards and requirements applied to US institutions and programs;
- *international program recognition*, which typically applies the general standards of accreditation, but does not confer formal status;
- *international consultation*;
- *free-trade and international reciprocity agreements*: paralleling the effects of the European Community's agreements on higher education, regional agreements in North America are beginning to pressure professional associations and their respective accrediting bodies to consider mutually acceptable standards. Five of the accrediting bodies surveyed reported that free-trade agreements have affected mobility in their professions, and nine had adopted international reciprocity agreements;

- *international licensure of occupations and international credential review*: of the forty-two agencies, seven reported international licensure, although this is usually limited to Canada.

Nevertheless, internationalization of the curriculum and the globalization of professions remain relatively new concepts, and discussion of the issues in the US has generally remained internal to professions or to the specialized accreditation community. Higher education is only beginning to grasp the powerful effect these changes will have on its future, although by January 1993 a major conference sponsored by the Center which the author directs on 'The Globalization of Higher Education and the Professions: The Mobility of Students, Scholars and Professionals' was attended by a broad constituency representing professional accrediting bodies, state licensure agencies, federal programs, and higher education institutions and associations from the whole of North America.

Regional Trade Agreements

As already suggested, the free trade agreements in Europe and North America are hastening the movement towards mutual recognition of professional qualifications. Since the initial signing of intent to create the North American Free Trade Agreement (NAFTA) in 1992, there have been many trilateral meetings among the higher education systems of Canada, United States and Mexico. Their task is complex since the three countries have strong state/provincial rights and a combination of centralized governmental (Mexico) and decentralized non-governmental (Canada and the United States) higher education systems. Many organizations and institutions have become involved in multiple linking activities to explore and promote trilateral mobility through conferences, projects and networks. Most notable is a joint initiative of the (Mexican) Secretaria Education Publica and the (US) Center for Quality Assurance in International Education towards the development of common educational standards for the primary North American professions.

International Higher Education Associations

International higher education associations also play a key role in advocating educational quality. The Fulbright educational commissions dotting the globe report increasingly of the need to develop quality assurance systems. The Canadian based Inter-American Organization for Higher Education, a non-governmental presidential association representing institutions of higher education in the western hemisphere, is an excellent example of how collaboration can promote educational improvement through its services and activities which cross all borders. And the International Network of Quality Assurance Agencies in Higher Education which generated the conference on which this book is based, is formed of associations, agencies and institutions responsible for assuring quality in many different countries, who have grouped together for mutual cooperation and information sharing.

International Assistance Organizations

Major international assistance organizations have identified higher education as critical to global development and are playing a significant role. In November 1992, UNESCO's International Congress emphasized the necessity for countries to pay attention to the need for quality assurance, and this was followed by regional meetings, such as one for the Ministers of Education of Eastern and Central Europe in May 1993. The World Bank has also made higher education and its quality a major interest, commenting.

> Complaints about the deterioration of the quality of higher education are common across the world; yet few countries have formulated specific performance goals for the sector. Targets for the level and quality of outputs from the system need to be set . . . Indirect interventions that have worked best include . . . quality assessment through peer review and accreditation (World Bank, 1990).

And together, UNESCO and the World Bank are discussing the development of a center for quality assurance in higher education in Central and Eastern Europe.

In 1990, the US Agency for International Development (AID) announced its new Agency Center for University Cooperation in Development, working through such programs as the University Development Linkages Program (UDLP). In 1992, this Center together with the American Council on Education and several other higher education associations, formed an Association Liaison Office to assist and sustain higher education quality in developing countries.

Internal Pressures for Quality

The demand for quality is also coming from within higher education systems, institutions and programs, as offshore provision and student mobility expands.

Exporting American Higher Education

From the belief that an international educational experience is intrinsically valuable and enriching has sprung the growing and often lucrative business of exporting higher education. The United States has exported an estimated 1,500 educational programs (not counting language programs). Two-thirds of these are study-abroad programs for American students; the remaining third are for foreign nationals. 300 institutions offer programs through 171 American military bases, and hundreds more offer a range of other degree-granting or credit-toward-degree-granting programs. For example, over thirty US institutions have established degree-granting activities in Japan within the last three years, and many are interested in starting programs in Eastern and Central Europe. New international links are being developed: several US institutions have contracted for example, to provide the first two years of a baccalaureate degree in Malaysia, with the last two years to be completed in the United States. Distance learning via telecommunications is extending institutional 'reach', and adding to increased problems of assuring quality for education which is not 'place based'. This is but a beginning. As the global recession continues, institutions from many more countries will seek to export their programs in greater numbers in order to secure additional revenues.

The American response to the quality assurance of this major exportation business has seen some progress over the last five years, but is generally slow and uneven. The intention is certainly that the regional and national accrediting bodies in the United States should be responsible for all educational programs of an institution wherever based. However, in practice they are not able to assure quality at all locations, particularly those overseas. In some cases, of course, they are not the responsible agent for quality assurance. For example, they have recently forfeited their role in evaluating programs on military bases to a process called MIVER funded by the Department of Defense and administered by the non-governmental American Council on Education. Language programs traditionally have not been subject to quality-assurance procedures since they have not been regarded as a credit-generating activity in American higher education. However, there is evidence that credit *is* being given on an increasing basis for these programs, and that their quality does need to be assured.

Another issue is the ability of institutional accrediting bodies to evaluate study-abroad programs. Steven Crow of the Commission on Institutions of Higher Education of the North Central Association of Colleges and Schools has commented,

> International linkages are not always strong educational linkages. Colleges link with free-standing profit and not-for-profit organizations that specialize in study abroad . . . (and) . . . several education ministries have begun to question whether US accreditation counts for very much when it puts its stamp of approval on such linkages. It is ironic that policy makers in Washington, DC rail against linkages in the US between profit and not-for-profit entities, but applaud such linkages abroad as a good way to encourage international economic development (Crow, 1990).

The growing problem of assuring quality in exported credit-generating or degree-granting programs and institutions (often called branch campuses) is of major concern, and in 1990 the institutional accrediting community developed a joint policy statement, 'Principles of Good Practice in Overseas International Education Programs for Non-US Nationals'. Despite this, at least one regional agency has seriously considered accrediting foreign institutions beyond the traditional scope of American-style institutions, located internationally but chartered in the US. And, to further exacerbate tendencies toward decentralization and fracture, in 1993 the Council on Postsecondary Accreditation, the umbrella organization of accrediting bodies, voted its own dissolution.

Importing Students

Many countries can boast growing international student populations. The United States now estimates it has nearly half a million students from other countries in degree-granting programs. Many of these, particularly those in graduate programs in technical areas, will enter the US labour force. The overwhelming majority, however, will return to their respective countries to assume positions of leadership.

International Quality Assurance

The growing export of education, combined with importing hundreds of thousands of students, has emphasized the need to assure the quality of educational products, leading accrediting bodies and international exchange organizations to develop principles of good practice and codes of ethics. The author's own organization, the Center for Quality Assurance in International Education, was established in 1991 with two primary objectives: one centered on the assurance of quality in the globalization of American higher education and the other on assisting other countries to develop a program of quality assurance for their own higher education systems. International organizations such as the Organization for Economic Cooperation and Development (OECD) are consulting through meetings and seminars on the principles of transparency, comparability and convertibility needed for an international approach to quality assurance in student mobility.

In the US and elsewhere there tends to be little coordination between those bodies formally charged with assuring quality in higher education and those which promote internationalization. The domestic process for assuring quality was not historically intended to serve an international purpose. On the other hand, the globalization of higher education is forcing it at least to consider matters beyond its borders. Whether we shall see comprehensive, international quality assurance processes within our own lifetimes remains in question. National and regional elements in the cultural, political and educational context are powerful deterrents to international collaboration. On the other hand, the globalization of higher education has promoted interdependence and links which will continue to grow. It behoves us to be responsive to assuring quality as the paradigm continues to shift.

References

CROW, S. (1990) 'Significance of international education ventures to the accrediting community', in LENN, M.P. (Ed), *International Education and Accreditation: Uncharted Waters*, Council on Post secondary Accreditation, Washington, D.C.

LENN, M.P. (1992) 'New paths to international mobility in the professions', *International Educator*, NAFSA, Washington, D.C.

LENN, M.P. (1992) *Quality Assurance in Higher Education: The Cornerstone of Development*, Center for University Cooperation in Development, US Agency for International Development. Washington, D.C.

NATIONAL ARCHITECTURAL ACCREDITING BOARD (1990) Unpublished survey, Washington, D.C.

WOODHOUSE, D. (1992) *QA Newsletter*, International Network of Quality Assurance Agencies in Higher Education, Hong Kong.

WORLD BANK (1990) *White Paper on Higher Education*, Washington, D.C.

Chapter 15

Overseas Franchising

Keith Short and Teo Chiang Liang

The Nottingham Trent University, UK, franchises some of its courses to a consortium of Malaysian Colleges. One author describes the franchising arrangements from the viewpoint of the University (the franchisor); the other gives the view of one franchisee (the private college of Kolej Bandar Utama). Some general principles and a framework for quality assurance of franchise operations are outlined.

Educational Franchising

Although there is extensive, often anecdotal, literature on franchising in the commercial and business world, there is very little on educational franchising — which is the teaching in one institution of courses designed and examined in another under the conditions specified by the franchising institution. Heger (1982) has reported on the potential benefits of franchising to small and medium-sized American colleges and Evans (1992) has given an example of how a university centre has been established in an area in the state of Minnesota in which there was no such provision. Descriptive accounts of franchising policies and practices in English polytechnics (now new universities) are contained in the report from a conference on *Franchising and Access: towards the identification of good practice* (NATFHE, 1991). The absence of public information is hardly surprising given the sensitivity of commercial information about an activity which has the potential to generate considerable income.

Nottingham Trent University (formerly Nottingham Polytechnic) is one of the largest educational providers in the UK with over 18,500 students, 700 academic staff, organized into eight faculties and twenty-seven departments, offering a wide range of academic programmes with strongly applied and vocational themes, and with well-established and well-tested quality assurance systems. Educational provision is available in flexible modes so as to encourage the widest possible participation. Learning at a distance in the home, in the workplace, or as an outcome of collaboration with other organizations in colleges and universities throughout the world is available. A range of academic links with over fifty institutions in the UK and overseas has been established which includes the franchising of the university's higher diploma, degree and postgraduate courses to be taught in other institutions.

The University considers that there is much educational value in franchising of courses for both participants, allowing the franchisor to expand provision at low cost at a time when there is capacity in colleges and limited opportunity for growth in universities, an opportunity to enter new regional and geographical markets and to strengthen international links, and an additional source of income. The franchisee gains a means of acquiring and delivering additional or new courses at least cost, an opportunity to enhance staff experience/development and quality assurance processes, and an additional source of income.

Assurance of Quality in Educational Franchising

The UK Business and Technician Education Council (BTEC), whose remit covers a range of post-school vocational programmes has clear guidance notes and procedures for the franchising of its courses (BTEC, 1991). However, the quality assurance arrangements for franchising between the higher and further education sectors have been more patchy. A report by Her Majesty's Inspectorate (1991) noted that although much teaching and learning in the colleges was of an appropriate standard, there was some less satisfactory work where colleges had little experience of higher education. Libraries were often inadequate, and management structures, quality control systems and liaison between institutions needed to be enhanced. In developing its own approach for the approval of franchising, the Nottingham Trent University has drawn on its established principles and practice of quality assurance. And from the experience of franchising courses to over twenty institutions, it has learned that a thorough and rigorous initial franchise validation minimizes the risk of serious problems later, especially with an inexperienced franchisee.

Whether the franchisee is located in the UK or overseas, a site visit is undertaken by a group of University staff with appropriate subject expertise and experience of franchising. The aim is to ensure that the franchised programme is comparable but not necessarily identical to that running in the franchisor institution, and that all students should be able to leave the programme having attained comparable learning outcomes. The exercise — however structured — has to establish the means by which the academic standards of the course will be maintained and must make sure that inter-institutional arrangements are understood with clear channels of authority and responsibility for action, preferably formally recorded in a 'memorandum of cooperation' between the franchisor and franchisee.

The University's validation panels seek to ensure that:

- the College has effective management and administrative arrangements for the delivery of its courses, with regard to the composition and function of course committees, responsibility for the maintenance of standards, and relationship and liaison mechanisms with the University;

- the resource base to underpin the course(s) is adequate and suitable, including physical accommodation, revenue and capital support, and academic and support staff;
- appropriate provision is made for staff development, research and professional activity for staff associated with the course(s);
- teaching and learning strategies are appropriate for the level of course(s) and that staff-development policies are in place to continuously develop course delivery styles and methods; and
- the course(s) is in an appropriate departmental/faculty and institutional context.

The University has selected academic partners in Malaysia who share its commitment to quality, sense of purpose and educational objectives. This partnership has been in operation for several years, and is centred on a consortium of five private colleges which are able to operate a university foundation course, seven BTEC Higher National Diploma (HND) courses and the initial years of two honours degree courses. To support this development the University has a member of its staff permanently based in Malaysia who coordinates the operation and delivery of courses, assists the colleges in staff-development activities, and facilitates information exchange.

The Demand for Higher Education in Malaysia

The Malaysian government realizes that the country's standard of living in the years ahead will depend ever more on the competitiveness of its industry and commerce. To achieve this, the Prime Minister has set the year 2020 for the country to be a fully developed nation. This ambitious undertaking is known to every Malaysian as 'Vision 2020.'

The Malaysian economy has been growing steadily at 8 per cent or more for the past five years and has a shortage of suitably qualified and trained human resources. The higher education institutions are unable to produce sufficient graduates to meet the needs of the economy, and the government recognizes the important role played by the private sector in filling the gap. This has led to a rapid growth of private colleges and a demand for foreign courses and training programmes to be conducted in Malaysia. In 1992, it was estimated that over 55,000 students were studying in private colleges at pre-university level.

As a developing nation, Malaysia believes it makes sense to look outside its borders for well-proven and tested courses and training programmes for its population. Malaysians would prefer to obtain internationally recognized diplomas and degrees and yet only a minority can afford to go overseas to achieve this. For this reason, many private colleges have collaborated with foreign universities and polytechnics to conduct their diploma and degree courses in Malaysia, whether in whole or in part. Kolej Bandar Utama, or in

English, First City College (FCC) is one such private institution, and its overseas links include collaboration with the Nottingham Trent University for the franchised use of some of its courses as described here.

The Link with First City College

FCC is currently franchised to offer the BTEC HND in electrical and electronic engineering, business and finance, and computer studies. HND graduates can if they wish continue their studies by pursuing the relevant degree courses in the University in one or two years depending upon the students' performance.

To gain franchising approval, the college first provides information about its mechanisms for internal quality control; review and evaluation systems; policy on resourcing; support for staff development; procedures for accrediting prior learning; procedures for appeals; equal opportunities policy; staff qualifications and experience; physical resources; and assessment strategy. Then several University staff conduct discussions in Malaysia with the chief executive officer, the principal of the college and the respective course leaders. This is a demanding and expensive exercise, and it is envisaged that the presence of the permanent University representative in Malaysia will help to streamline the process. There are inevitably cultural and other differences between the franchisor and franchisee institutions. For the franchisee to operate at the same level as a long-established franchisor is a daunting task, and flexibility in the imposition of the conditions of approval is needed, particularly at the initial stage.

An important aspect of the link concerns staff development as FCC needs to be exposed to, and updated on, the teaching methods and the assessment strategy used by the franchisor. Here the University has arranged for FCC staff to visit the University to see at first-hand the teaching methods and equipment used, to attend course committee and examination board meetings and to exchange ideas with the University lecturers. University staff also regularly travel to Malaysia to conduct meetings and workshops for FCC staff.

The course structure and syllabuses are entirely the University's, but certain modifications, particularly the writing of case studies which reflect local conditions and experience, are made to suit the Malaysian environment, subject to the University's approval. Some difficulties are encountered here, though they are not insurmountable. Data, statistics and other primary sources required for the writing of cases are not as easily available as in the UK and, where available agencies may not be very willing to release the information.

The College has been generally satisfied with the level of academic support provided by the University, and feels that direct dealings with the respective departmental heads and senior staff have been effective, even though the distance and other pressures on staff means the response time may sometimes be slow. Areas covered concern the details of syllabuses to be taught, the extent and depth of knowledge of each subject to be covered, the type of equipment to be purchased by FCC, and the evaluation of applications from students requesting exemptions from certain subjects. The University's staff member stationed in Malaysia is the eyes and ears of the University, with the right to visit FCC at anytime during business hours and to talk directly to FCC staff and students, and helping FCC by resolving some queries quickly and assisting with the implementation of validation conditions.

The link with the University has helped to formalize and strengthen the quality assurance methods that FCC already has in place. New methods and procedures of quality control have been successfully introduced. FCC students appreciate the efforts to provide quality education, and the introduction of student representation on course committees, though a new and revolutionary concept in Malaysia, gives students the opportunity to voice their opinion. The academic staff are proud to be teaching quality courses in a quality conscious environment despite the workload. Staff development opportunities include encouragement to pursue postgraduate studies and add to their motivation.

In setting the validation process and standards, costs must be borne in mind so that the saving to Malaysians in pursuing franchised courses at home is not eroded, defeating the main objective. Good quality assurance is probably rather more expensive than many currently believe. From the viewpoint of the franchisee it is an investment considered to be entirely necessary to ensure the quality and standard of the education offered to students. However, for any collaborative arrangement to succeed, give and take is essential. Difficulties will arise, and when they do, the partners have to seek solutions together which are acceptable to both, as has so far been achieved in the international franchising arrangement described here.

References

BTEC (1991) *Franchising: A Guide to Partnership in Programme Delivery*, London.

DES (1991) *Higher Education: A New Framework*, Cmnd. 1531, London, HMSO.

HEGER, H.K. (1982) 'Revolution in small colleges', *Educational Record*, 63, pp. 18–19.

EVANS, G. (1992) *Franchising Higher Education: The Rochester Community College experience of building a University Centre*, Coombe Lodge Report 22, pp. 749–66.

HMI (1991) *Higher Education in Further Education Colleges: Franchising and other Forms of Collaboration with Polytechnics*, Department of Education and Science Report 228/91/NS, London.

NATFHE (1991) *Franchising and Access: Towards an Identification of Good Practice* (1991), Report of a Conference, London.

Chapter 16

Transnational Distance Education

Kay J. Kohl and Gary E. Miller

The authors describe the rapid increase of transnational distance education through the growth of electronic media of instruction. The chapter focuses on the implications for higher education institutions and their staff and students, and suggests some strategies for ensuring the quality of this educational provision.

The Growth of Transnational Distance Education

Whereas in the past colleges and universities have been accused of thwarting distance education, today many are becoming involved because of the growth of electronic instruction. Complete master's degree programs in engineering and business are available electronically. Nurses, teachers, and law enforcement personnel are also among those turning to distance education to acquire courses needed for recertification or to complete a baccalaureate degree. No longer is electronic instruction solely a solution for dispersed rural populations. It is fast becoming a practical alternative for urban residents who value convenience.

Several forces are currently advancing this development. For one thing, public institutions, forced to adjust to state budget cutbacks, are looking for ways to deliver education as efficiently as possible. The demand for higher education opportunities is expanding as life-long learning becomes a necessity for more working adults struggling to adapt to a rapidly changing economy. Meanwhile a growing segment of the population is comfortable acquiring knowledge electronically. (In the US in 1992, 72 per cent of households had VCRs and at least 20 per cent had home computers. And the Clinton Administration is urging the development of high-speed national computer information networks to link schools, businesses, hospitals and governments across the country.)

It does not require a great leap of imagination to predict that before long many higher education institutions will be deciding whether, and under what conditions, to make their electronic instruction available transnationally. Already many students seek graduate and professional continuing education outside their home country. Should these programs become more accessible worldwide via electronic instruction, it is easy to foresee a sizable international market emerging for such products.

Kay J. Kohl and Gary E. Miller

Utilization of advanced communications technologies promises both to extend universities' reach and to change their approach to instruction. Already some institutions are offering 'virtual university' telecourses. For instance, a graduate course for mid-career managers developed by New York University's School of Continuing Education involves the instructor and students in a collaborative online learning experience designed to teach students how to analyse, design and build 'corporate cyberspaces' for their own and case-study organizations. Even though the instruction, administrative services, and library resources are all accessed electronically, the virtual university system is highly interactive and facilitates frequent communication among students and the instructor. The new communications technologies can enhance education, provided that universities are prepared to break away from old models and reconceptualize how they teach. With both learning and teaching systems in flux as a result of technological change, it is essential that the approaches to quality assurance devised for transnational distance education anticipate evolution and not impede the development of university electronic instruction.

Given the present and projected expansion of electronic distance education, higher education governments and quality assurance agencies need to rethink how quality is assured. In the United States for example, higher education institutions are subject to governmental and non-governmental quality control. Neither of these systems appears up to the task of assuring the quality of transnational distance education. States set standards for institutions that operate within their boundaries. The six non-governmental regional institutional accrediting bodies use their own criteria to evaluate institutions in a particular geographic area. There are no generally accepted national standards for distance education or for the international activities of U.S. colleges and universities. It is a quality assurance system devoid of any international perspective. In short, there are no explicitly stated guidelines that could help assure the quality of transnational distance education offered by US institutions.

Why Quality Assurance Has Become an Issue

For Higher Education Institutions

Internationally, distance education is often associated with specialized national institutions designed to serve adult students. Many of these are modelled after the very successful Open University of the United Kingdom. For open universities, the primary concern is not simply to overcome distances, but to design organizational structures and programs around the needs of working adult students. Distance education in the open university context is critical to the entire institution and this reality defines the relationship between an open university and its students.

In the United States, most distance education is conducted by colleges and universities in which the focus remains on traditional instructional programs.

Many of these providers are comprehensive institutions whose reputations derive from the production of high quality graduate education and research, and whose faculty members see themselves primarily as researchers. Electronic distance education is still a relatively new phenomenon in these institutions and they are concerned about how it might influence their hard-won institutional reputations for academic quality. Because distance education programs can be highly visible to the general public and to peer institutions, they are not without risk for the institution.

Recently, distance education has attracted the attention of state governments for several reasons. First, many states are moving toward the development of state-wide telecommunications systems for distance education. A recent legislative report noted that all fifty US states have some kind of distance education network in development. Also, legislators and state educational regulatory agencies have become interested in distance education as part of a larger concern for institutional accountability. States are seeking to hold the higher education institutions which are supported with taxpayer dollars, accountable for the quality of education that the institutions provide. In some states, this has resulted in new, stringent reporting requirements for public universities and the tendency to isolate distance education for special oversight. This latter trend could impede efforts of universities to utilize advanced technologies creatively for instruction and could slow development of transnational distance education.

The rapid development of new distance learning media and software, offers institutions access to a wealth of interdisciplinary materials and international course alternatives. Increasingly, this places institutions in one country in the position of having to decide whether to take advantage of high quality, easily available materials produced elsewhere or to invest time and resources in the development of their own products.

For Academic Staff

Newer interactive technologies, such as compressed video, have helped to reduce faculty resistance to distance education. Still, concerns about how staff are rewarded for their involvement in distance education persist. Developing new software for electronic instruction tends to be a time-consuming and often undervalued endeavour for an academic. Tenure decisions attach more importance to research than teaching, let alone distance teaching.

Complicating the quality issue is a new, unanticipated form of peer review that can occur with certain kinds of distance education. In many distance education programs, staff not only teach but also serve as the authors of the accompanying text materials. When these instructional materials begin to reach far beyond the geographic area normally served by the institution and/or are adopted by other institutions, academics soon discover that their distance education work is subject to a kind of peer review usually reserved only for their scholarly research writing.

For Students

For students, access has been the first and foremost issue, and a distance education program has quality by virtue of the fact that no other option is available. When a student's options increase, however, so may the student's criteria for defining quality. How does the use of various media contribute to the learning process? What are the trade-offs? What are the weaknesses relative to a traditional instructional environment familiar to the student? What support services are available? How well are distance learning programs accepted by employers and by other universities?

Increasing numbers of students appear willing to combine some distance education with on-campus courses, especially when it facilitates progress towards a degree. For example, staff and students in universities outside the United States are relying on video courses developed by US institutions to pursue additional advanced studies in subjects that would otherwise not be offered by their home universities.[1] This acceptance of electronic instruction assumes that institutions will count courses delivered electronically towards an academic degree or the licensure requirements of a given profession.

Possible Strategies

With transnational university distance education still in its infancy, this seems an excellent time to identify quality assurance strategies. The primary concerns can be grouped loosely into collaboration issues, academic policy issues, and intellectual property issues.

Collaboration Issues

Most institutions become involved in transnational distance education through a consortium. Costs make that a practical option. There is no single consortial model, however. As more colleges and universities have acquired an electronic distance education capacity and moved to utilize a variety of new technologies — including Hypertext, multimedia as well as videotapes — these institutions have created diverse consortial structures to respond to their particular objectives.[2]

Sometimes universities will agree to license their courses to one or more institutions abroad. For such an arrangement to succeed, there needs to be a high level of trust established among the educational leaders involved in the partnership. Institutions leasing their courses want assurances in advance that the receiving institutions will use their courses responsibly. Institutional reputations are at stake. The threat of distortions is real insofar as an institution in another country will often need to amend and/or translate distance education courses to better serve local audience needs. The institution which is concerned about the possible misuse of one of its courses by an institution in another country always has the option to decide not to lease it. Often, however, potential misunderstandings can be avoided by establishing good communication channels.

With the rapid growth of transnational distance education, colleges and universities need to assume new quality assurance responsibilities. Originating institutions must stand behind the academic quality of the instruction which they sell to other institutions. Similarly, receiving institutions must be prepared to review course materials critically for both content and cultural appropriateness before agreeing to incorporate them into their own curricula.

Internationally, graduate-level and professional short courses are those that are in greatest demand when it comes to electronic instruction. More universities around the world are moving toward a three-tiered degree system (bachelors, masters, and doctorate) and there is mounting interest in master's degree programs offered on a modular basis. This promises to facilitate the reciprocal recognition of credentials and acceptance of courses by universities in different countries. Many institutions already have the requisite technology in place and are eager to access the graduate-level courses of other countries. Such collaboration can offer important two-way benefits; institutions can access cutting-edge courses offered by top international experts. No country has a corner on the expertise in every subject. Transnational distance education gives an institution the possibility to tap other nations' academic talents and offer its students advanced instruction in subject matter which might otherwise be unobtainable in the country.

Colleges and universities which lease courses created by institutions in other countries often decide to translate the video courses, but there are real advantages to offering the course in its original form. In the case of the United States, where only a small percentage of university students ever study abroad, the opportunity to take courses in one's field of concentration from a first-rank scholar of another country in another language could both increase students' foreign language proficiency as well as their knowledge of a given subject. While satellite transmissions from a university in another country would never be a substitute for the study abroad experience, they could provide an inexpensive way for more students to interact with their counterparts in another country on a regular basis and in so doing, help to expand the participants' global awareness.

Higher education institutions are encouraged to forge cooperative distance education course-exchange agreements with universities in other counties. The goal should be to provide students with the opportunity to enrol directly in courses offered by institutions in diverse countries and apply those credits to degree studies in their home institutions.

Academic Policy Issues

The main purpose of academic policy is to ensure quality of instruction. An institution planning to deliver its courses to students internationally or to distribute course materials to institutions abroad, faces a number of new academic policy issues.

The academic standards of courses delivered transnationally should be comparable to counterpart courses offered at the home campus. Students must be confident that their credit will not only transfer but that the knowledge gained from a course will prepare them for subsequent courses. The courses themselves must have comparable treatment of subject matter. An institution must decide, as a quality issue, whether it is appropriate to teach exactly the same content both at home and internationally. It may decide, for instance, to tailor the course content to the background and experience of students in a given country. The ability of students to understand local references and cultural perspectives may affect their ability to learn effectively. And, if the course is adapted to the international context, the developer must be confident that the adaptation has not weakened the instructional design of the course.

Institutions planning to market their distance education courses abroad have a responsibility to ensure that the materials work well in other cultures. This applies regardless of whether an institution is enrolling international students directly or sharing its materials with institutions in other countries. One measure that an institution can take is to involve international curriculum advisers in the development of course materials to ensure that the content will be suitable for an international student audience. Wherever possible, a course should incorporate international case studies and readings so as to offer a global perspective on the subject. Finally, those preparing the course should be encouraged to search for relevant, internationally-developed media materials that can be utilized in the course.

In the very near future, it can be anticipated that there will be increased demand for professional, graduate-level credentials that have international validity. A case in point is environmental engineering. Already the prospect of a North American Free Trade Agreement coming into force is prompting discussions among educational leaders in the United States, Canada and Mexico. They see transnational distance education as a way to rapidly train the many engineers and inspectors who will be needed to implement the environmental provisions of the agreement. Meanwhile at a trilateral meeting of educators from the three NAFTA countries in September 1993, it was recommended that the trading partners work to strengthen economic links by establishing a North American distance education university. It is envisioned that this new institution would award graduate degrees based on a composite of approved courses provided electronically by participating universities in the three countries.

Institutions involved in distance education need to take substantial responsibility for program quality. Typically, this involves establishing a peer review system to evaluate the quality and effectiveness of the course instruction and computer software exported transnationally via distance education and, where relevant, ensuring that the instruction takes account of accepted international standards relative to professional practice. Ensuring student progress is a central concern: institutions seeking to offer credit for electronic courses to international students abroad must arrange to provide the relevant academic advisory, testing, and administrative services. Regardless of the instructional delivery mode, a college or university should be held responsible for the quality of the instruction that it provides, and should not seek to avoid this responsibility by 'tagging' (i.e., by distinguishing a course on a student transcript by delivery mode).

Intellectual Property Issues

Distance education involves a variety of intellectual property issues, often interacting with course design concerns. At the most basic level, institutions intending to offer courses transnationally or to make instructional materials available to other institutions internationally should ensure that all copyrighted materials contained in the course are properly cleared for use in the intended countries. This is a design issue, as the availability of international rights may affect the selection of resources included. Similarly, staff should try to select textbooks that either have international editions or that are readily available internationally. Ideally, those responsible for developing a course should avoid tying it too closely to a single text, so that alternative texts can be used if necessary.

Printed materials can present a serious problem in transnational distance education. Even if the materials are suitable, economic differences may make it impractical to simply sell books published in an industrialized country to students in developing countries. Solutions to this problem, such as arranging for in-country duplication or electronic customization, raise a variety of copyright difficulties. The way for institutions to surmount them is to minimize the use of third-party copyrighted materials in distance education courses. If use of certain books is necessary to ensure the academic quality, the institution should as a part of its course development budget invest in securing the worldwide rights or at least ensure that worldwide rights are available at a reasonable cost. Similarly, when negotiating with course authors and content experts, it will be in the institution's interests to retain control over the transnational distribution and revision of the instructional materials that it owns and intends to export.

Conclusion

The transnational distribution of college and university electronic instruction is at hand. As more nations seek ways to access electronic instruction, advanced computer software, and digital libraries internationally, it is of critical importance to institutions, faculty and students that mechanisms be developed to assure quality. The purpose of these mechanisms should be neither to impede the international dissemination of electronic instruction nor to hinder the development of collaborative educational networks. Rather the goal must be to capture the promise of transnational distance education by pursuing strategies that will promote quality education, facilitate international cooperation, and encourage effective use of scarce resources.

Notes

1   For instance, the University of Wollongong in New South Wales, Australia, has arranged to purchase a number of engineering courses from American engineering schools through the National Technological University. Wollongong is using some of these courses to develop its own engineering masters' degree programs. Moreover, it plans to re-broadcast these courses to some fifteen other Australian universities, which are part of a national engineering distance education consortium in that country.

2   Common consortial models found in the US include the following:

- *Single Institution with Collaborative Sites*
  Some institutions use distance education to offer their degree programs on a national basis. For example, the University of Arizona delivers a master of library science degree to students in eleven states. UA relies on cooperating institutions in those states to provide on-site support services. In this particular consortial model, an instructional mentor at the collaborating site is central to quality control.

- *External Degree Program Supported by Multiple Institutions*
  This consortial model offers students the opportunity to take courses offered by various consortium member institutions and apply them towards a degree granted by a single consortium member. An example of this kind of organization is the National Universities Degree Consortium which involves ten large US public universities (Colorado State University, Kansas State University, the University of Maryland, the University of New Orleans, the University of Oklahoma, Oklahoma State University, the University of South Carolina, Utah State University, Washington State University, and California State University — Long Beach).

- *Inter-institutional Consortium*
  The National Technological University (NTU) is perhaps the best example of this model. The forty-five engineering schools involved in this satellite network contribute courses to NTU and several inter-institutional expert faculty committees are responsible for determining and reviewing the curricula for each of NTU's ten established master's degree programs (computer science, computer engineering, electrical engineering, engineering management, hazardous waste management, radiation health physics, manufacturing systems engineering, material science, management of technology, and software engineering). NTU courses are licensed by institutions outside the US, provided the institution responsible for originating the course consents.

- *Resource-sharing Consortium*
  A resource-sharing consortium develops and produces various distance learning instructional resources for its member institutions. The Interna-

tional University Consortium (IUC) at the University of Maryland is an example of this kind of consortial arrangement. IUC serves as a kind of library for the institutions in its international membership. They turn to the IUC for a variety of instructional materials, which they then incorporate into their own courses.

Chapter 17

The World Bank Contribution

Paul Hebert

The World Bank is actively involved in higher education. As a financial lending institution, it stresses efficient use of scarce national resources. The author outlines the Bank's policy in promoting greater reliance on private financing of higher education institutions, and in providing assistance to maintain and improve quality in the public and private sector.

The World Bank is no stranger to education, especially higher education. It is not only interested in the 'bricks and mortar' component of education, but has a keen concern for quality, and this at all levels of the sector. It has always been interested in performance and standards within the sector, and an on-going concern for efficiency and cost effectiveness in all its education projects reflects its strong views on the need for quality improvement and assurance.

The World Bank and Education

The value of human capital development has been a major factor in the role that the Bank has exercised in the area of international development. Whether in the formal educational system or in the broad variety of non-formal educational activities, the Bank has consistently maintained that the development of human resources is a major priority in promoting growth in developing countries.

The Bank's portfolio includes an important component for education, in 1992, for example, totalling 8 per cent. On a regional basis, Latin America and the Caribbean have been the largest recipient of loan assistance (42 per cent). Then followed East Asia and Pacific (25 per cent), Africa (21 per cent), South Asia (8 per cent), and the Middle East and North Africa (4 per cent) (World Bank, 1992). Since the political upheavals in eastern Europe, this region has also received considerable aid for education (Harbison, 1991). Assistance has been provided to all educational subsectors, with priorities being adjusted in keeping with the new factors and circumstances arising on the international scene. As mentioned above, all such assistance was provided with a vital concern for cost effectiveness and efficiency — and for an improvement in the quality of the education offered.

The World Bank and Higher Education

The Bank has exercised a prominent role in supporting the development of higher education systems in Asian, Latin American, Caribbean, Middle Eastern and many European countries since 1963. A total Bank investment of more than US$5 billion has been provided for 281 higher education projects with 432 higher education components. This amount represents 37 per cent of lending for education during the period 1963–1991 (Eisemon, 1992). Investment in higher education has increased from an average of 17 per cent of all education lending in the 1960s, to 37 per cent since 1986.

The Bank involved itself in loans for higher education at a period when many countries of Africa, Asia, and the Caribbean were gaining independence and seeking to develop rapidly bureaucracies to manage public investments which were intended to stimulate economic growth. In the period 1963–1975, 61 per cent of higher education lending supported universities. Beginning in the early 1970s, the rationale for such large donor and government investments was questioned. Analyses of rates of return demonstrated that developing countries were 'over-investing' in higher education and that resources should be re-allocated to primary education (Eisemon, 1992).

This shift was encouraged in Bank educational research and policy statements throughout the 1970s and 1980s. Various policy papers (World Bank, 1971; 1974) suggested more emphasis on primary and even non-formal education and criticized the disproportionate directing of resources to secondary and higher education. Bank investments to universities decreased between the mid-1970s and mid-1980s (World Bank, 1980). However, since then, because the total volume of lending has gradually increased, higher education's share grew from 30 per cent to 43 per cent. In effect, the competing requirements of higher and primary education have been accommodated by the growth of assistance for education in general (Stevenson, 1991).

Geographically, investment in Middle Eastern, European and particularly in East Asian countries has grown more rapidly than lending to Africa or Latin America and Caribbean nations. In the most recent past — 1986–1991 — East Asian countries, principally China and Indonesia, have accounted for 33 per cent of project investments and nearly half (47 per cent) of higher education lending (Eisemon and Kourouma, 1991).

Bank lending for higher education has been geared to institutions which train teachers (to facilitate expansion of school enrolments) or which train technicians for the productive sectors. Approximately a third of higher education investments has supported teacher training and 24 per cent has been directed to polytechnics or technical-training institutions. On the other hand, support for national scientific institutions which are responsible for advanced training and research is very recent. Together with universities, where most scientists and engineers are engaged in the developing countries, bank lending to such institutions between 1986 and 1991 has amounted to 46 per cent of project investments and 58 per cent of higher education lending.

Despite this relatively increased attention to higher education, there is a consensus that the subsector is facing a crisis, especially in developing countries. This involves rapidly increasing enrolments in a context of diminishing resources to support such growth, poor quality, unemployment of graduates, inequity in national resource allocation, and a political paralysis in educational reform (Salmi, 1991).

While the crisis is ascribed to various causes, these mainly relate to the role of the State. In many countries, the intervention of governments in the development of higher education was required in order to supply the rapidly expanding public sector with highly trained personnel. Private investment was either inadequate or politically undesirable due to concerns with equity. However, conditions have changed in ways that now require serious re-assessment.

Many Bank education policy makers today believe that solutions to the crisis involve a better relationship between the growth and distribution of higher education enrolments and the national labour market, and a greater reliance on private financing to increase investment in higher education. In effect, it is felt that state involvement should become more selective and less direct.

In many countries, high-cost universities account for an unnecessarily large proportion of enrolments. Open universities, polytechnics, community colleges, long and short-cycle technical institutions should be looked to as viable low-cost alternatives. Frequently, graduates of such institutions have better employment opportunities and are often more diverse in gender and socio-economic composition.

In many countries, private institutions absorb a large proportion of higher education enrolments, whereas in others such institutions are either tolerated but have no legal basis, or are completely proscribed. The World Bank believes that governments should encourage the development of private higher education so as to manage better the growth of public institutions, to encourage diversity in training programs and to broaden social participation in the subsector (Ziderman, 1990). Inevitably, such a development would require mechanisms to foster quality improvement and assurance and to provide subsidies to private institutions and/or to their students.

States would need to exercise supervision to encourage quality improvement in the private sector, and would need to undertake measures to improve quality in the public education sector also. In the context of the serious financial constraints that confront most developing countries, increasing financial support to improve quality is not a viable option. Funds for developing quality can only come from diversification of the financing of public higher education; institutions themselves must assume responsibility for this diversification by reducing their reliance on State support, and can achieve this

- by seeking to recover a higher proportion of their unit costs from tuition fees;

- by reducing non-instructional expenses; and
- by generating more income from private sources, e.g., continuing education programs, contract research, consultancy services, etc.

In turn, however, these same public institutions will need to have greater control over the factors that affect their costs and over the funds that are raised and utilized. To encourage the accountability that would need to be assumed by the institutions, mechanisms for the allocation of resources to the public institutions have to be transparent, must provide incentives for efficiency, and must permit flexibility.

The need to diversify public institution funding and the valuable contribution of private education have been two important perspectives that characterize the current Bank policy. The Bank sees this strategy as a concrete measure that makes potential quality improvement a possibility. By seeking to diversify its funding of public higher education and by developing a partnership with the private sector, newly available government resources could be directed to efforts at quality improvement and assurance.

The World Bank and Quality Improvement and Assurance

Despite the difficulty of defining quality, professional educators have gradually evolved a number of standards to evaluate whether or not quality exists in a particular educational activity. Whether it be in programs, professors, and students or in physical facilities and support services, norms have been identified and subsequently utilized to determine quality. Obviously, these have been and need to be constantly examined and reviewed to assure that they reflect new findings of educationists and the demands and needs of our changing societies.

The maintenance and application of such norms have been the responsibility of professional bodies composed of educators, administrators, and other interested social scientists. These groups have assisted parents, institutions, governments, and others in identifying quality norms and organizing the process by which the latter can be quantitatively measured. In many cases, professional bodies subsequently give their stamp of approval, i.e., accreditation. The role they have played and continue to exercise is critical in dealing with the issue of quality in education, but especially in what concerns its improvement and assurance.

While by statute and constitution the Bank has no right to claim itself an educational institution in the normally accepted connotation of the term, it nevertheless is in a position to exert meaningful influence in the search for educational improvement. By its very status the Bank is limited in the nature of the influence that it can exercise. It will not for example deal directly with individual educational institutions in a particular country. By statute it can only operate via its respective national government members, and its major point of possible intervention lies with the government of a country, usually with a particular ministry or department as the contact point. Thus if the Bank wishes to involve itself in the process of quality improvement it must seek to accomplish this in collaboration with government.

Constraints frequently arise in dealing with government and the situation often is even more tenuous in the case of developing countries; despite the efforts of many colleagues esteemed and respected for their integrity and high professionalism, the ugly head of nepotism, incompetence, and opportunism often rears itself and adds to endemic bureaucratic procedures and policies. In spite of these constraints, the Bank still believes that government constitutes a key instrument in the process of quality improvement. How best then can the Bank function in exercising its influence? How can it maximize its input to the process of educational improvement in a particular country or region?

In the view of the Bank, the role of government in higher education must change. It can no longer assume sole responsibility for providing, financing, and managing that subsector, but must develop a partnership with the private sector (Geiger, 1988). In addition, for that component of higher education which remains in the public domain, government must strive to develop alternatives to the current practice of full support. It is in the context of these two perspectives that the Bank believes that it can exert an important influence, in terms of long-term quality improvement and assurance.

The private sector in many developing countries is strong and actively contributes to providing a large proportion of post-secondary training. In the Philippines, for example, approximately 86 per cent of higher education is handled by private institutions. In Brazil, Indonesia, Bangladesh, and Colombia 60 per cent of university education is provided privately. There are private colleges and universities in at least six francophone and anglophone countries. In most instances, a long colonial tradition accounts for such a situation (Eisemon, 1992). In the former socialist countries of Central and Eastern Europe there is a nascent private sector. Hungary, the Czech and Slovak Republics, Poland and Romania are all exploring private initiatives. Given that public sector financing will be significantly decreasing, private institutions and private financing can play a crucial role in this region. The private sector has been most dynamic in those states which enjoyed a comparatively higher level of prosperity and more contact with Western Europe in the socialist period, particularly Hungary and the Baltic States. A good example of the latter is Lithuania's Vytautas Magnus University in Kaunas, reopened after a hiatus of forty years, whose core undergraduate curriculum emphasizes computer science and English-language training. The university is well managed, has recruited qualified staff, and offers relatively low-cost programs that appear to be closely related to emerging employment opportunities. However, in the majority of developing countries, post-secondary education is exclusively public, or if a private system does exist it is relatively small and most frequently weak.

In many instances, the very legal status of the private sector is not clear or is totally non-existent. In encouraging government to recognize the valid partnership that could exist, the Bank can assist in funding the improvement or development of the legal structures, and is currently involved in doing this in several eastern European countries.

While a program of state subsidies would be desirable, many governments are not in a position to provide this and the private sector is expected to be able to support itself. However, even in this situation the Bank may be in a position to assist. For example, it is in the process of developing an initiative in Cameroon whereby Bank lending would be used by government to establish a national, private-education development-assistance fund. Such arrangements, though not provided by the Bank, have functioned effectively in El Salvador and the Philippines.

Although an effective sharing of responsibility with the private sector for higher education can be beneficial, government cannot divest itself of its role of supervision nor shed its responsibility for improving such a sub-system.

As for public post-secondary education, government financial constraints can no longer cope with the burden entailing full support of state institutions. Uncontrolled enrolment growth, the proliferation of academic programs, overly generous student scholarships, and heavily subsidized student services have resulted in government having limited or no resources to commit to improvement of educational activity within the institutions. The consequent deterioration of educational efforts in many institutions has reached critical proportions. For example, there is now considerable agreement that the quality of university education is deteriorating across sub-Saharan Africa (Saint, 1993).

The Bank believes that more money to continue such high-cost but low-quality educational activity is counter productive. The solution, it feels, lies in government having state institutions assume greater responsibility for contributing to diminishing their per capita student costs. Government can introduce tuition costs and fees, and encourage institutions to reduce non-instructional expenses, and to generate more income from private sources. Concomitantly these same institutions will need to be given more control over factors that affect their costs and the utilization of funds raised. The savings in state subsidies so generated could then be allocated to measures that could directly affect change geared to the improvement of quality, e.g., research, library resources, laboratory equipment, instructional materials, faculty/staff development, etc.

In discussing lending for reform of the education sector with various governments, the Bank has introduced the concept of this type of shift, and has provided funding for the technical studies needed to introduce such innovations. More and more countries are including such steps to change as part of the reform of their educational system. Through its funding the Bank can play a catalytic role in promoting meaningful change and can subsequently contribute to improvement in the quality of the education process and its product. Being in a position to provide funding for such change, the Bank can exert vital influence in encouraging government to be concerned about the quality of its educational efforts. Here too, when shifting much responsibility for financial viability to institutional efficiency, government cannot shirk its task of the appropriate supervision concerning the quality of the education system's efforts.

The effective exercise of this is no easy task. Understandably, institutions of higher learning, both public and private, believe that they know best how to carry out the academic and administrative functions that will contribute adequately to graduates' personal welfare and that of the nation. Appropriate and meaningful institutional autonomy can coexist together with effective government oversight. However, government often needs assistance in maintaining a proper balance in meeting its responsibility of supervision. Is such assistance available to government? Who can provide such professional help?

Fortunately, the need for such assistance has been recognized both nationally and internationally. Individual educators and professional organizations and associations have sought to make such help available. Many developing countries and individual institutions have had recourse to them when addressing themselves to the issue of quality improvement.

Again, the Bank can provide needed assistance to government, via its framework of lending policies, mechanisms, and procedures. It has encouraged governments to collaborate with professional groups, and has funded technical assistance which enables governments to call on their services. Evaluative norms are examined and adapted as national circumstances require, and evaluation mechanisms developed to assist government in carrying out its appraisal of institutional efforts (Joni, 1989). In some cases, funding mechanisms are introduced as incentives to institutions interested in improving their professional performance. These initiatives allow government to engage in meaningful supervision and evaluation, while respecting institutions' autonomy. Implemented in a professional and collaborative manner, such activity can effectively contribute to system-wide and institutional improvement. Recent experience in Kenya suggests that the contribution of the private higher education subsector is more positive when government develops a regulatory framework providing appropriate accreditation criteria, technical assistance for curriculum development and management, and financial incentives to support the development and qualitative improvement of private higher education institutions.

Over and above the assistance that the Bank can provide to governments of developing countries, it collaborates actively with numerous national, regional, and international groups in their efforts to exert greater and more effective influence on national systems and individual institutions, as well as with professional organizations concerned about quality improvement and assurance.

Conclusion

Basically a financial lending institution, the World Bank has nevertheless stressed the necessity of efficient utilization of scarce national resources, especially those committed to development of people via education. In emphasizing cost effectiveness in national educational expenditures for higher education, the Bank has always encouraged government to consider improvement and assurance of quality a major objective.

To this end the Bank encourages government to recognize the contribution of the private sector to strengthening the national education system. Furthermore, it provides financial and technical assistance to help governments foster a shift from total support of post-secondary education to having public institutions take on a greater responsibility for their operational and professional activity. The new thrust to shared responsibility subsequently renders available funds to be committed to quality improvement.

References

EISEMON, T.O. (1992) 'Lending for Higher Education: Analysis of World Bank Investment 1963–1991', Washington, D.C., World Bank.

EISEMON, T.O. (1992) 'Private Initiatives and Traditions of State Control in Higher Education in Sub-Saharan Africa', Washington, D.C., World Bank.

EISEMON, T.O. and KOUROUMA, M. (1991) 'Foreign Assistance for University Development in Sub-Saharan Africa and Asia', Paper Presented to Senior Policy Seminar on Improvement and Innovation in Higher Education in Developing Countries organized by the World Bank, 1–4 July, Kuala Lumpur, Malaysia.

GEIGER, R.L. (1988) *Privatization of Higher Education: International Trends and Issues*, International Council for Educational Development, Princeton, N.J.

HARBISON, R. (1991) 'Human Resources and the Transition in Central and Eastern Europe', Washington, D.C., World Bank.

JONI, T.R. (1989) 'Creating the Foundation for National Accreditation of Teacher Training Program's in Indonesia: The Second Indonesia-IBRD Teacher Training Program Institutional Self-Study and Peer Evaluation', Paper presented at the Annual Meeting of the Comparative and International Education Society, 31 March–1 April, Cambridge, Mass.

SAINT, W.S. (1993) 'Universities in Africa: Strategies for Stabilization and Revitalization', Technical Paper No. 194, Washington, D.C., World Bank.

SALMI, J. (1991) 'The Higher Education Crisis in Developing Countries: Issues, Problems, Constraints, and Reforms', Paper Presented at the 1991 Course on Sociology of Science, Inter-University Centre, Dubrovnik, Yugoslavia, May.

STEVENSON, G. (1991) 'Adjustment Lending and the Education Sector: The Bank's Experience', Washington, D.C., World Bank.

WORLD BANK (1971) Education Sector Working Paper, Washington, D.C.

WORLD BANK (1974) Education Sector Working Paper, Washington, D.C.

WORLD BANK (1980) Education Sector Working Paper, Washington, D.C.

WORLD BANK (1988) *Education in Sub-Saharan Africa: Policies for Adjustment, Revitalization, and Expansion*, Washington, D.C.

WORLD BANK (1992) *Annual Report*, Washington, D.C.

ZIDERMAN, A. (1990) 'Universities and Development: The Evolving Role of the World Bank', Paper Presented at the Annual Conference of the Comparative and International Education Society, Anaheim, California, March.

Chapter 18

Comments from UNESCO

Marco Antonio Rodrigues Dias

UNESCO's perspective on quality in higher education is presented here. Quality assurance is seen as a priority, while recognising that developing countries which most need to enhance the quality of their provision have least resources to do so. The UNITWIN/UNESCO Chairs Programme is described as an attempt to disseminate expertise and encourage international collaboration.

To define quality is not an easy task and there is no common agreement on this subject. However, when UNESCO was preparing its medium-term plan for 1990–5, it held a series of regional consultations and international meetings to formulate the main concerns for higher education, and the two groups of issues identified everywhere were:

- issues relating to relevance (role of higher education within societies, democratization, need for diversification, links with the world of work, responsibilities of higher education in relation to the whole system of education etc.); and
- issues relating to quality (reforms and innovations, including distance education, interdisciplinarity and continuing education, planning and management of resources, organization of programmes, qualification of teachers etc.).

These two sets of issues were complemented by suggestions and proposals concerning mobility and the strengthening of international cooperation in the field of higher education.

Efforts in North America, Western Europe and elsewhere to enhance educational achievement and develop national standards and assessment panels are matched by activities in Eastern Europe, Latin America and Africa. For example, recently CEPES, UNESCO's European Centre for Higher Education in Bucharest, proposed the creation of a European Group on Academic Assessment reflecting:

- the concern for quality instruction, as evaluated against certain standards of excellence;

- the expansion of international cooperation and academic mobility, both of students and of staff; and
- the need for accreditation to define how institutions (mainly new institutions in Eastern Europe) should be approached, and how the public or other interested institutions should regard them both from the perspective of educational policy and from that of present or future students.

The aims of the Group will be:

- to make a comparative analysis of criteria and procedures of evaluation of higher education;
- to facilitate the development of compatible criteria for excellence within the European systems of higher education; and
- to further develop the means of implementing the UNESCO Convention on the Recognition of Studies, Diplomas and Degrees.

At a special meeting CEPES organized in 1993 for ministers of education from Central and Eastern Europe, the participants approved a set of recommendations, the first one being related to quality:

The issues of quality assurance, assessment and improvement, as well as those of institutional accreditation should be closely linked to the processes through which higher education systems and institutions are being reformed, by means of appropriate policies and mechanisms of implementation (UNESCO, 1993a).

Similar statements resulted from UNESCO Meetings organized recently by CRESALC, the Regional Centre for Higher Education in Latin America and the Caribbean which is located in Caracas, and by BREDA, the Regional Centre for Education in Africa, located in Dakar, Senegal.

UNESCO's View of Quality

On the basis of its regional discussions, UNESCO's Division of Higher Education prepared a draft policy paper in which there is an important section dedicated to 'Quality in Higher Education'.

The demand for increased relevance in higher education goes hand in hand with the demand for its enhanced quality. Quality is not a novel concern in higher education, but it has become crucial in present policy debates concerning the development and reform of higher education. It embraces all its functions and activities: quality of teaching, training and research — which reside in the quality of its staff and of its programmes and resources; quality of learning — as a corollary of teaching and research, but also implying quality of students;

quality of governance and management — which has a determining impact on the teaching, learning and research environment.

Quality of Staff

Higher education institutions, primarily universities and other university-level institutions, enjoy great prestige on the national and international scene. This prestige is assured principally by the eminence of their teachers and researchers. It would be a great misfortune if universities anywhere were to fall into disrepute. However, it would be equally counter-productive for higher education institutions to take prestige and privileges for granted. Everywhere in the world, government leaders, politicians, representatives of the corporate sector and of public opinion at large, insist on the fact that quality in any kind of institution — academic institutions included — cannot be assured without a mechanism of evaluation, quality assessment and control.

The evaluation process should start with, and actively involve, the academic and research staff, given their central role in the diverse activities of higher education institutions. Clearer policies and practices are needed for staff development in higher education. They should be based on initial and in-service training for this purpose, including pedagogical training, and on more rigorous mechanisms for access to, and selection for, university teaching. Accountability and evaluation — through self-evaluation, peer-evaluation, or external evaluation — are increasingly being recognized by the academic and administrative staff as essential to assuring the quality of their institutions.

Quality of Students

Participation in tertiary-level education has shifted from being a 'reflection' of social and economic relationships to being a determinant of such relationships and the overall development of society. Higher education plays an increasingly important role in ensuring upward social mobility. Equity calls for greater opportunities for members from lower-status groups to participate in quality educational programmes. The possibility for young people to pursue higher education studies is not only important from the point of view of higher educational institutions. Society makes long-term investments in higher education not only for economic reasons. Cultural development, the building up of more cooperative and participatory relations in society are directly related to the level and quality of education.

There is every justification to consider students as a great asset of society. However, with the advent of mass higher education, it is necessary to engage in a serious debate on a number of basic issues concerning access to higher education. Current UNESCO estimates indicate that there will be some 120 million young people seeking higher education by the year 2040. Most of them will be in the developing world. Thus, increasingly pertinent will be such policy questions as: Can a trend toward increasing access be upheld indiscriminately? What could be the mechanisms allowing societies to afford mass higher education in order to observe the principle of social equity?

One of the key issues seems to be related to the ways in which governments can offer the institutions of higher education and their future graduates incentives to become partners in the overall effort of national development, not only beneficiaries of public support. The interrelation between secondary education and higher education and between the latter and various forms of continuing education acquires particular importance in this respect.

Quality of Governance and Management

A clear understanding of relations between higher education and the state are a precondition for quality and accountability in governance and management in higher education institutions. The principle of academic autonomy is central in this respect. Academic freedom and university autonomy guarantee the preservation of the university as a community of free inquiry and the stimulating climate required for scientific advancement and dissemination of knowledge. Governments should accord the proper degree of autonomy — together with adequate financial provision — to higher education institutions in order to allow them to be relevant and perform their creative, reflective and critical functions in society. Therefore, the evaluation and quality assessment should not be perceived as a restrictive instrument for allocation of resources, but the process allowing higher education its self-improvement.

However, institutional autonomy also implies increased responsibility in matters of funding, systematic self-evaluation of research and teaching and a constant concern for cost-effectiveness and efficiency in all activities. It also requires, as emphasized above, greater interaction between higher education and society which should be based on partnerships and alliances with a wide range of economic, social, cultural and other public organizations.

Analyses of the present conditions of higher education are unanimous in pointing to insufficient financial resources as one of the main constraints for its further development. The challenge of limited resources is unlikely to be overcome in the near future. Thus it will be necessary for higher education institutions to show a capacity to redress themselves in order to be able to cope with this challenge. Elimination of weaknesses in governance and management is paramount in this process. Therefore it is in the interest of higher education that it considers the issues of evaluation and quality, including institutional and programme accreditation, as being vital for a responsive and accountable system of governance and management. The most viable institutions of higher education, also in financial terms, are those which have succeeded to build into their functioning structures, proper mechanisms allowing them to remove mediocrity and to guarantee quality of teaching, research and service. They are also the institutions which stand a better chance in the competition to secure resources from the public and private sectors' (UNESCO, May 1993b).

Universities and Societies

Universities do not exist in isolation: external forces have a tremendous impact. It is not possible, for example, to study the financial situation of universities in developing countries, without making an analysis of the consequences they suffer from debt and structural adjustment policies. In fact, universities are embedded in their societies and many of their problems are the reflection of the changing world.

As a consequence, before defining the new missions of the universities in present times, it is absolutely necessary to define the kind of society and the kind of international order we want to build. Economic development cannot follow rigid structures and only one model for all countries and regions. The failure in the strategies of cooperation based on the transmission of models, as has been done in Africa for example, with old colonial systems, suggests that this approach is not a good one. In all regions, the adoption of foreign concepts and values and the neglect of regional and national cultures and philosophies have had negative repercussions on the higher education systems. The reforms of higher education systems in Latin America at the end of the 1960s and in the 1970s based on foreign models was a failure that policy makers are now trying to correct by adopting new reforms based on the specific situation of each country. In other words, quality in concrete terms cannot have the same meaning in San Francisco, Paris, Frankfurt, Ouagadougou, Cuiabá, or Gaborone.

The UNESCO draft policy paper continues:

the higher education institutions are called to carry out their functions in a very quickly changing world. The end of East-West ideological divide, the worldwide demand for the practical recognition of human rights, the serious struggle for the abolition of apartheid, the progress of democracy, the restoration of authority of the UNU system, give greater faith in the action of the international community to tackle, in a spirit of solidarity, the major challenges of today's world: hunger, disease, poverty, homelessness, unemployment, ignorance, the protection of the environment, the construction of peace, the consolidation of democracy, the respect of human rights and the preservation of the cultural diversity. All this calls for a rethinking of the missions of international organizations like the United Nations system, and, at the national level, of institutions like the university'. And in the fulfilment of its constitutional mission, to 'maintain, increase and diffuse knowledge . . . by encouraging . . . the international exchange of persons active in the field of education, science and culture, UNESCO relies on higher education and the academic and scholarly community as a major partner in action (UNESCO, 1993b).

The same document proposes a basis for a model of a new society:

The basic premises of the concept of indigenous and sustainable development were formulated by the United Nations in its International Strategy for Development (IDS, 1991) which was approved by the General Assembly of UNO. The IDS considers that economic development should be based on two main foundations; diminution of poverty and development of human resources. With regard to the latter, the universities and other higher educational institutions have become, more than ever, the main actors in the implementation of the strategy for development, particularly with regard to their role in the training of highly qualified personnel.

The search for solutions to global problems is the responsibility not only of governments, but of each community, individual and citizen. Two of these problems can be considered as the main ones in present times — the environment and peace. The United Nations Conference, held in Rio de Janeiro in 1992, confirmed, once again, that the environment is part of human development. It also showed the direction to follow in all major areas of environment and development — the Agenda 21. The Agenda for Peace, a document presented by the Secretary-General of the United Nations in 1992, is a true plan of action for peace which coincides with the basic principles of the 'culture of peace' that UNESCO promotes through its programmes. The Charter of the United Nations and these documents are the basis for a new international order. These are also the foundation for the development of an agenda for action based on three great pillars: non-violence, equality and liberty. These should also be the basis for establishing the link between learning, research and civic responsibility. They should also constitute the bedrock for the renewal and strengthening of the links between the university and society (UNESCO, 1993b).

To democratize the access and keep a high level of quality in the services provided to societies are the main challenges higher education institutions face today. Some analysts, looking at institutions which have not been able to adapt themselves to new situations, have concluded that the increase in enrolments has given rise to expenses which cannot be met by states' budgets, and that it has generated social inequities, because the wealthiest people have been privileged. This can be true in some parts of the world or in some institutions, but the analysis risks going too far if it concludes that developing countries should not invest in higher education. This is not acceptable. Without a good higher education system, developing countries will not overcome the barriers for improving quality of life, and will become dependent for ever. With the end of the strained relationship between East and West, the main problem in the world is underdevelopment and the strengthening of universities for training and research is essential for its solution.

The educational system constitutes a whole: if a part does not operate properly, the whole will generate dysfunctions. Higher education is responsible for training managers, experts and researchers necessary for development. Deleting resources at this level, can represent a dead-end for real independence in many countries. And it is not possible to reinforce primary and secondary education without a good system of training at the higher level. Teachers in primary and secondary schools need to be trained and they are mainly trained in higher education institutions, which are also, in several countries, the only institutions able to provide educational research, essential for policy makers to take valid decisions.

UNESCO's Action

While UNESCO developed this kind of reflection and policy, the Organization decided to launch in October 1991 the UNITWIN/UNESCO Chairs Programme. This is intended to enhance the capabilities for advanced training and research and contribute to the development of know-how for the rapid transfer of knowledge to developing countries. The UNITWIN/UNESCO Chairs Programme basically involves the creation, in partnership with universities and other international bodies or funding agencies, of professorships enabling visiting scholars to provide core expertise for the development of centres of excellence in key disciplines and in the fields related to sustainable development.

This initiative completed a series of other UNESCO actions, which have implications for quality in higher education. Among the more important ones were six regional conventions on the recognition of studies and diplomas in higher education which led to an international recommendation on this topic.

Practically each and every institution of higher education claims that it is, if not the best, at least in the same category with the best. Each institution takes it for granted that its diplomas and degrees should be automatically recognized, while the degrees of other institutions need careful scrutiny before assessing their comparability and possible equivalence.

The obvious solution would be to copy and reproduce everywhere those models of higher education establishments which are considered to be 'the best', to have replicas of Oxford and Cambridge, of Harvard, Stanford, Berkeley or MIT, of the Sorbonne, Salamanca, Coimbra and Heidelberg or anywhere else in the world. But any such listing, however long, will always leave people unsatisfied. Why Oxford and not, also, London and Edinburgh? Why Heidelberg and not also Geneva or Lausanne etc. But this is not the real issue. The consequences of that approach whereby many African higher education institutions, established according to the models of the universities in the metropoles were devoid of relevance for their countries have already been mentioned. Universities in Eastern and Central Europe — some of them of long-standing tradition — lost their vitality under the impact of an imposed model which was created to suit the needs of totalitarian regimes, and many Latin American universities spent their energy trying to impose a model which was not adapted to their needs.

The value and strength of higher education resides in its worldwide diversity. All UNESCO Regional Conventions on the recognition of studies, diplomas and degrees, underline the richness and diversity of the national systems of higher education as a most important asset which must be preserved and further promoted. Quality and relevance of higher education institutions, of their programmes and their diplomas, cannot be judged in terms of given models, however perfect they may seem. They must ultimately be assessed in a particular context, and at a given time.

It would be gratuitous and untrue, on the other hand, to make the reverse claim that all higher education institutions are equally good and therefore the recognition of their diplomas and degrees should be taken for granted. Adopting this standpoint would mean avoiding a discussion of the real issues facing higher education today some of which are raised here with particular reference to the need for increased international cooperation as a means to assure quality.

The Demographic Factor

Third level education has been expanding constantly from 28.2 million in 1970 to 47.5 in 1980 and 58.4 in 1988. The number of third-level education students can be estimated at about 65 million at present. For the world of education, the second half of the twentieth century will remain in history as the period of the most rapid expansion of higher education. Higher education is the most dynamic level of education at present and will continue to be for the foreseeable future.

Current estimates, (and they are rather conservative) indicate that some 120 million students will be seeking higher education qualifications by the year 2040. Most of these will be in the developing world. Are the decision-makers, the university leaders, the professoriate ready for this situation? Dumitru Chitoran, of the Division of Higher Education of UNESCO, stated in one internal meeting in May 1993:

> UNESCO can only support and very strongly indeed, the need to give a chance for accomplishment to the talented young minds every-where and more particularly so in the developing world. But this optimistic approach must be accompanied by affirmative action on behalf of all those concerned to assure quality of higher education when large numbers are involved. I believe that we can subscribe to Eric Ashby's statement that 'more' does not necessarily mean 'worse', but it certainly means 'different'. Higher education everywhere — in the industrially developed countries and in the developing ones — must change. They must build into their functioning structures operative mechanisms allowing them to remove mediocrity and to guarantee quality.

The Widening Quality Gap in Higher Education

The deteriorating socio-economic situation of the developing countries, par-ticularly of the least developed ones, leads to the continuous aggravation of the crises of their systems of higher education. There are institutions of higher education in Africa and elsewhere which face imminent extinction, unless urgent steps are taken to rehabilitate them.

A very serious vicious circle has been created. On the one hand, eco-nomic growth and development in general, has become increasingly dependent on knowledge and on its application. In the knowledge intensive societies of today's world, attempts to bridge the gap between the industrially developed countries and the developing ones necessarily call for people with high-level knowledge and skills. This need has turned the universities and higher edu-cation institutions into key factors for human development. And it is precisely there where this function is so much needed, namely in the developing coun-tries, that they are least equipped to perform it.

The difficulties facing higher education in the developing countries call, in the first place, for appropriate measures and efforts to be made by the respective states themselves. However, beset as they are with serious socio-economic problems, bearing the burden of foreign debts, these countries will not find it easy to allocate significant resources to higher education. Interna-tional assistance to developing countries to enhance their high-level training and research capacities has become essential for human development in the

South, precisely because it is only in that manner that continued dependence on foreign assistance can be diminished and finally stopped.

University Development Aid

The main aim of the UNITWIN/UNESCO Chairs Programme is to assist higher education institutions in the developing world to enhance the quality of their teaching and research programmes, and to rehabilitate their facilities. By contributing to quality assurance, UNITWIN also brings a contribution to the mutual recognition of studies and degrees.

A genuine academic, while primarily concerned with the quality of his/her own institution or department, must be equally concerned about the quality of higher education institutions everywhere. It was this strong confidence in world academic solidarity that guided the Programme proposed. Some of its main features are:

- *Transfer of knowledge and competitiveness in higher education*
  One laureate of the UNESCO Kalinga prize used simple language to express a very meaningful thought: Science must be like the sun; it should shine for everybody.' Universities, by virtue of their academic freedom and autonomy, are fully committed to the pursuit of knowledge and to its dissemination as the very essence of their scientific role. Liberty of research goes hand-in-hand with the liberty to share the results of research, if knowledge is to advance. On this matter, UNESCO approach is different from that of other organizations, which look for the concrete benefits 'donors' get from cooperation. UNESCO looks for solidarity, for a policy of sharing resources. The role of competitiveness in the pursuit of knowledge should not be neglected. Without competition acting as a stimulant, progress is slowed down. But there is healthy competition which can only be welcome for universities everywhere, and there is fierce competition which necessarily leads to the final destruction of the weak.
- *A more even distribution of 'centres of excellence'*
  The very concept of 'centre of excellence' has direct implications for the recognition of studies and qualifications. The world of higher education has changed considerably as a result of its massive expansion. No university can claim to be 'excellent' in every field. But certain universities manage to maintain an aura of 'excellence' by tradition, by myth or simply by better advertising. Others, which are equally good, have still to win international recognition. It took two Nobel Prize winners in a row (Claude Gille de Genes and George Charpak) for the *Ecole Nationale de Physique* in France to impose itself as a leading research centre in the field.

What is at stake here is that each higher education institution must aspire to excellence in at least some fields. And one way to do it is through inter-university cooperation, resulting in a sort of 'division of tasks', preferably trespassing national frontiers. It is one of the aims pursued through the UNESCO Chairs. They are conceived to function as centres of advanced studies and research, located at a particular university, primarily in the developing world, but extending their services to institutions in the respective country and subregion. An interlocking system of international chairs can make an important contribution to the overall enhancement of the higher education institutions in a given (sub)region. It is one way by means of which South–South cooperation in higher education can be promoted and an important contribution that the institutions of higher education can make to the Technical Cooperation among Developing Countries (TCDC) Programme of UNDP.

- *Rehabilitation of universities in the developing countries*
  To render these institutions competitive in the world academic scene and thus to gain recognition of their diplomas and degrees, an all-out concerted effort must be made so as to reverse the decline in quality of their teaching and research programmes and of their facilities. International cooperation cannot be the entire answer, but it can make an important contribution towards reaching this goal.

The UNITWIN/UNESCO Chairs Programme has in mind precisely those institutions of higher education which are in greater need of support. The Director General was persuaded that the governments of the industrialized countries, the inter-governmental organizations, the various donor agencies and foundations were ready to respond to UNESCO's appeal. But he relied in the first place on the spirit of solidarity of the world academic community. 'What is needed is a large-scale movement of university volunteers' whether they be dedicated scholars ready to impart their knowledge to those who are mostly badly in need of it, together with colleagues in the developing world and thus enrich their life and scientific experience, or technicians who could help with the maintenance of university facilities and laboratory equipment. They are needed in great numbers and the exemplary success of the UN volunteers or of the *Médecins sans frontières* leads UNESCO to believe that the academic community will respond in a similar manner.

Conclusion

Quality cannot be derived from a universal model, quality cannot emerge from theory and abstraction, quality is the result of a series of actions responding to precise social needs in a very particular moment. Real quality is *hic et nunc* (here and now).

Guy Neave has commented caustically that 'quality' has now been added to the 'Gladstone bag of universal problems' and that 'academic life finds itself beset by a growing and often cacophonous crowd of quality assurers'; he concludes that 'the issue behind quality has very little to do with 'quality'. It has to do with who sets the criteria involved in its definition and from these to the question of control over the heart of the academic enterprise is but a short step'. He adds: 'Quality, seen from this angle, is a technique which allows national administration to insist on the ends whilst rigorously denying the means.'

Guy Neave touches a real problem. When international experts try to impose a model on the developing world, they are not helping quality per se, they are serving the creation of mechanisms aiming to control the development of endogenous capacities. They don't serve liberty, they serve the spirit of domination and of control.

UNESCO is a human organization and as all human achievements is not perfect. As an international organization with more than 160 member states, it has the qualities and the imperfections of those who compose it as an entity and who establish its principles and decide on its orientations. But, UNESCO, as the whole United Nations system, is not a simple addition of parts, it plays in the world an ethical role in calling attention to global values and stimulating a spirit of solidarity. In practical terms, as far as higher education is concerned, UNESCO tries to develop a permanent reflection on the main issues affecting systems and plays a catalytic role using its moral authority and its presence in all parts of the world for establishing and reinforcing links among the academic community and among institutions themselves. UNESCO considers the internationalization of knowledge as a condition for the development of all countries. To reach this target, quality linked to relevance is essential and universities, through teaching and research, should serve their societies. These are UNESCO's guiding principles in the field of higher education.

References

NEAVE, G. (1993) Editorial in *Bulletin* of International Association of Universities, 4, 1, February.

UNESCO (1993a) Recommendations arising from a CEPES Conference on Quality Assessment and Institutional Accreditation in Higher Education, Oradea, Romania, May.

UNESCO (1993b) Draft Policy Paper on Higher Education, May.

Chapter 19

Trends and Issues

Diana Green

Agencies which assure quality in higher education vary in status, scope of operation and focus of attention; they also have some common features. Some of the issues addressed here are the nature of quality, the notion of 'stakeholder', quality assurance methods and procedures, and the growing burden for institutions. Quality profiles are suggested as a way forward.

Trends

That quality in higher education is important is taken as axiomatic. What is more difficult is the task of making any meaningful generalizations about trends and issues. This is partly because it implies that there is some consensus in defining quality, and about the nature and purpose of quality assurance, and about how and by whom it should be operated. The task is made more complex because higher education throughout the world is undergoing substantial restructuring. In consequence of this transformation, and of the differential rate of change, there are significant differences within and between countries in respect of the individual missions and organization of institutions delivering higher education, and the policy and value systems in which the institutions operate. These in turn affect the arrangements by which the quality of higher education in individual countries is controlled, audited and assessed.

Increasingly institutions are expected to make a contribution to economic, social and cultural progress. In some measure this has always been understood as their role, but now funding is being closely related to performance against specific targets geared to this end, and accountability has become the keynote of government/higher education relations. This is a relatively foreign notion in higher education, where activities have been sheltered from questioning eyes by the traditional defence of 'academic freedom'. It is symptomatic of, and provides a rationale for, the recent upsurge of interest in quality in higher education which has its origins in:

- widespread concern about the size of public expenditure and the share of higher education, especially in the face of competing demands such as health, social welfare, or other levels of education;

- the problems associated with the expansion of student numbers, resulting in a proliferation of types of institution offering higher education. Diversity of 'mission' raises legitimate questions about quality of output ('does different mean worse?'), especially when budgetary stringency means that expansion can only be achieved with a shrinking unit of resource ('does more with less inevitably mean worse?');
- demands for increased accountability which in some countries are a product of an ideological commitment to make public services, including education, more efficient and more responsive to the needs of customers; and
- the internationalization of higher education — the expansion of mobility for students, teaching staff and researchers, together with the internationalization of the labour market have highlighted the need for greater transparency about the nature and equivalence of academic and professional qualifications, especially as far as employers are concerned.

Quality Assurance Agencies

Although accountability is one of the characteristics common to quality assurance, the nature of agencies taking responsibility for assuring quality in higher education differs from country to country. They vary in

- status, notably whether owned by, or independent of, the institutions whose quality assurance procedures are being scrutinized;
- in scope of operation — some focusing narrowly on the quality of teaching, others with a remit extending to include quality of research and institutional management; and
- in the focus of attention, which may be a particular aspect of teaching quality (the discipline or the programme of study) or, more generally, institutional effectiveness. To some extent focus is determined by whether the agency sees its task as primarily oriented towards accountability or quality improvement.

Despite these differences, there are a number of common features. Whatever the focus of attention, the methodology appears to incorporate the same three ingredients, involving a judicious mix of subjective and objective data through self assessment, statistical or performance indicators, and peer evaluation, normally in the shape of an institutional visit. Paradoxically, inspection, which involves direct observation of teaching and learning as a central element of the evaluation process seems to have been virtually eliminated[1].

A second common feature is the growing openness and transparency attached to the quality assurance process. It is increasingly the norm that reports of the findings of external agencies are published. Publication is seen as a mechanism which both meets the accountability requirement and also promotes quality improvement.

Issues

What Quality?

This issue has both a conceptual and a practical dimension. If we wish to assure, control, assess, manage or improve quality, we must initially define it. While much has been written about quality in education, little has been written about the concept itself. Many commentators have pointed to the paradox: that while we all have an intuitive understanding of what quality means, it is often hard to articulate. Some have refused to engage in the discussion of what quality is, citing by way of justification the fate of Phaedrus in Pirsig's novel (who went crazy when he found a single substantive definition) (Pirsig, 1976). Others have taken a more pragmatic and epistemologically more viable approach by defining quality as 'fitness for purpose' (Ball, 1985; Reynolds, 1986; Brennan *et al.*, 1992). One recent attempt at analysing different ways of thinking about quality in higher education contrasts this functional definition of quality with conceptualizations which see quality as exception, perfection, value for money and transformation (Harvey and Green, 1993).

There are three variants of the exceptional notion of quality: the traditional notion of quality as distinctive, quality as excellence, and quality as passing a set of required standards. The traditional view is associated with distinctiveness, something special or 'high class'. This approach underpins the elitist view of the high quality of an Oxbridge education in the United Kingdom, or in the Grandes Ecoles in France. This is not quality to be judged against a set of criteria. It is exclusive, and apodictic (one instinctively knows it). The traditional view in education is that universities embody quality. They do not need to demonstrate it. The system is not exclusive but quality is self evident. There are no agencies specifically charged with the task of quality assurance.

The second variant often uses excellence interchangeably with quality, which it sees either as high standards or zero defects. It is about excelling in input and output: if the best students are lectured by Nobel Prize winners, the results may well be excellent.

The third variation dilutes the notion of excellence, focusing rather on the definition of a 'quality product' as one that has passed a series of quality checks. These checks are based on attainable criteria that are designed to reject 'defective' items. In this version, quality is attributed to all those items that fulfil the minimum standards set by the monitoring/inspecting agency. Quality is thus the result of 'scientific' quality control, it is conformance to standards. Hotel and restaurant 'star' ratings and final degree results in universities provide examples of such quality ratings.

The standards approach to quality offers both a method of external quality control, but also a framework for quality improvement since it implies that quality is improved if standards are raised. This approach assumes that standards are 'objective' and static (Walsh, 1991). In reality, standards are subject to continued renegotiation, a fact which is undermining the traditional view of final degree classifications, in the United Kingdom, as a 'gold standard' against which performance may be measured (Alexander and Morgan, 1992).

A separate but related question is what aspect of higher education should be the focus of quality assurance activity? In principle, there are several options:

- inputs to the teaching and learning process (e.g. human and physical resources);
- the process itself;
- outputs (the number of graduates, their employability, the standards achieved, the knowledge, skills and attitude they acquire);
- the individual institution and its (quality) management;
- the discipline; and
- the course/programme of study.

The decision will rest on the interest of the individual stakeholder. Thus, governments and employers are likely to be most concerned about the outputs of the higher education system, while students are more interested in the inputs to the learning process and the process itself.

Whose Quality?

The shift from the traditional exceptional notion of quality to the definition of 'fitness for purpose' has had two important and related consequences. First, it breached the traditionally producer-dominated culture of higher education by introducing the idea that quality might be defined in terms of the extent to which it meets the specifications of the customer. Second, the attempt to sort out who is the customer led to the realization that, in higher education, there is no single customer but a multiplicity of customers or stakeholders. Thus, the service user (the student) is as much a customer as those which fund the institution (the government, the taxpayer, the employer). This necessarily complicates the task of meeting the customer's needs: which customer should have priority? Taking the view that the student is the key customer raises a number of difficulties, not least the fact that in the education process (unlike manufacturing industry) producers and consumers (lecturers and students) are both involved in the production process. Nor does defining quality in higher education as meeting customers' needs necessarily imply that the customer is always best placed to determine what quality is or whether it is present. Indeed, where customer (= student) satisfaction is incorporated into institutional quality assurance procedures (Mazelan *et al.*, 1991), it is essentially the proxy assessment of quality based on the declared levels of satisfaction of the students. Students have very little information on which to make quality comparisons and, in practice, do not draw links between satisfaction and quality (Roberts and Higgins, 1992). Moreover, in fulfilling the requirements it sets itself, the course (or the institution) mediates students' expectations and affects their satisfaction accordingly (Lloyd, 1992).

An alternative view of fitness for purpose avoids the issue of determining who are higher education's customers by returning the emphasis to the institution. In this case, quality is defined in terms of the institution fulfilling its own stated objectives or 'mission'[2]. Quality becomes fitness for, and performance in, the market as perceived by the institution. This view of quality underpins the approach of the British Government which (post-1992) seeks to ensure that the new funding arrangements for teaching should be 'related to and safeguard the best of the distinctive missions of individual institutions' and is reflected in the methodology underpinning the two main external checks on quality, audit and assessment.

The focus on institutional effectiveness rests in many instances on a definition of quality which relates it to *value for money*. There is growing pressure on higher education institutions to demonstrate their efficiency and effectiveness *inter alia* by managing expansion without a comparable increase in resources and with no decline in quality (or standards). It is therefore not surprising that a key issue today is whether quality should be 'protected' by making funding conditional on its presence, adopting methodologies for funding teaching which reward quality and penalize unsatisfactory provision. This raises questions of both principle and practicality:

- should there be such a link between quality and funding?
- who should assess the quality?
- how should quality be assessed?

Methodology

Stakeholders will only have confidence in the quality of higher education (whatever the focus of their interest) if they have confidence in the methods used to demonstrate that quality (however defined) is present. This suggests that quality assurance methods must be transparent, robust, reliable, credible and demonstrably effective. Perhaps one of the reasons for the continuing pressure on higher education institutions to justify their existence can be found in the failure of the existing quality assurance arrangements. This 'failure' is attributable to three related factors: the methodology is complex, potentially open to abuse and not demonstrably cost effective. Moreover, there is a singular lack of evidence that these cumbersome procedures have had any impact on the quality of output.

As already indicated, the three common elements which underpin the practice of quality assurance in general use are institutional self-appraisal, performance indicators and peer review, in some cases involving a visit by 'peers' external to the institution whose quality is being assessed. The use of self-assessment reflects the conviction within higher education that the most reliable safeguard of quality and standards is not external controls but the development of the institution as a self-critical academic community. The major difficulty with self-assessment is that it is subjective. It also frequently lacks rigour. Peer review is open to a similar charge, even though it may incorporate elements which appear to demonstrate greater 'objectivity' (e.g. the use of performance indicators or, in the case of visits by teams external to the institution, people representing groups outside the academic community, such as employers). In addition to subjectivity, the major methodological weakness of peer review is its unreliability (Harvey, Burrows and Green, 1992). Peer review based on team visits is also problematic. Reviewers have been found to be biased as a result of their educational, social and institutional background (Blumer and Sinclair, 1973). Different peer teams have been found to be inconsistent in their judgment (Healey, 1980). Moreover, peer review visits may be perceived to be self-serving, especially if subject specialists predominate in the panel (Davis and Stronz, 1985). Peer review has primarily been used, irrespective of the focus of attention (i.e., on systems or subjects), to ensure threshold quality rather than to make comparative judgments about the provision of subjects, programmes of study or institutions. Indeed, it is questionable as to whether peer review is an effective method of making comparative judgments, given the qualitative nature of the judgments involved (despite its extensive use in the assessment of research proposals and academic publishing). While performance indicators provide an 'objective' counterweight to the criticisms of peer review and self-assessment, they too have methodological weaknesses which have been thoroughly rehearsed elsewhere (Harvey, Burrows and Green, 1992). In addition, a number of charges have been identified relating to their use in quality assurance, such as interpretation, the risk that priority will be given to objectives which are easily measurable (Sensicle, 1991), and the charge that their use may lead to unanticipated and undesirable behaviour.

An underlying concern is the danger inherent in over-reliance on self-regulation: 'Quis custodiet ipsos Custodes?' — (Who is to guard the guards themselves?). Can the external quality assurance procedures operated by agencies 'owned' by and accountable to, the universities which established them be demonstrably effective? This must be an important consideration for those countries currently exploring the different models currently available as they design their own external quality assurance systems.

The question of ownership is essentially another dimension of the issue about objective information. This raises again the related issue which is perhaps one of the most controversial aspects of accountability: comparative judgments about quality (of institutions, subjects or programmes of study) and the publication of 'league tables'. The underlying logic is clear: stakeholders have a right to information about the quality of the services provided by higher education. In the case of students and employers, that right extends to information about the differences in quality between institutions. This takes us back to the issues of how quality is defined and assessed. If the principle of comparability is difficult to challenge, there are genuine problems about how effectively this might be done.

There is some interest (evidenced in the literature) in quality assurance and quality management techniques developed outside of higher education, such as Total Quality Management (TQM) or industrial models of quality assurance based on standards (such as BS 5750 or IS 7000). Both models are principally concerned with improving the quality of products by the careful identification of customers' needs and decreasing the degree of variation in the production process, thus reducing waste and rework. The aim is to have quality 'built in' rather than inspected and a vital prerequisite is that quality is seen as the responsibility of all employees involved in the enterprise. However, although TQM may have 'already arrived in higher education' in the USA (Marchese, 1991), it appears to have made little headway in Europe.

Prima facie, there are some potential attractions of such systems. Internationally recognized quality management systems, especially those which confer a 'kitemark', provide a means of communicating with stakeholders outside of higher education judgments about quality and standards in a language they understand. The primary focus of TQM on the customers' requirements provides a healthy counter-balance to the traditionally producer dominated culture of the educational sector. TQM also provides a mechanism for managing cultural change within the organization. It is therefore useful for institutions wishing to shift the value system towards a greater interest in and concern for, the continuous improvement of teaching quality.

The relative lack of interest in these industrial models may not just be symptomatic of the scepticism of universities to the relevance of the concepts and practices derived from profit-oriented private organizations. While academics do manifest a tendency to believe that 'higher education is different' and to reject potentially good ideas on the grounds that 'they were not invented here', there are arguably practical difficulties relating to the need to accept a definition of quality based on customers' needs, as discussed previously.

Models derived from the manufacturing sector may also prove inadequate to the task of quality improvement, especially the improvement of the 'service encounter' (i.e., the students' experience). This is a problem education shares with other public and private services. It adds force to the hypothesis that rather than looking to manufacturing, higher education should look to the service sector for alternative models of quality assurance (Parasuraman et al., 1985). These approaches tend to place greater emphasis on those issues central to quality improvement such as the character of the service encounter and recognition that service quality will be a balance between the expectation of the customer and their perception of the service received (such that a 'high' quality of service is one where the customers' perceptions meet or exceed their expectations).

However, the academic culture is highly resistant to the notion of 'customers' for both philosophical and practical reasons. Moreover, education is not a service for a customer but an ongoing process of transformation of the participant (student or researcher). The problems associated with this approach to quality lie beyond the scope of this paper and have been discussed elsewhere (Harvey and Green, 1993).

The Burden of Quality Assurance

The final issue is easy to describe if difficult to resolve: increasing pressure for accountability presents a growing burden for institutions. This is exemplified in the increasing number of external agencies with a right to call for information about, and proof that the quality of teaching is being maintained and improved. At a time of declining resources, the need to get the right balance between the demands on academic staff of responding to (and, through peer review, participating in) external quality assessment and the need to invest, *inter alia* through research and scholarship, in the continuous improvement of the students' experience is paramount. The problem becomes potentially greater as higher education becomes increasingly international in scope. One nightmare scenario involves institutions being confronted with external scrutiny by teams not only from five or six domestic stakeholders, but also their regional and international counterparts!!

The Way Ahead?

A model of quality assurance might satisfy the requirements of accountability within a wider international context, should acknowledge that:

- accountability means that institutions must be open to external scrutiny and that the outcomes of that scrutiny should be published. Better communication means that reports must be in a form which is open to, and comprehensible by the various stakeholders;
- quality improvement is the responsibility of the institutional provider of educational services. Quality management is facilitated by external scrutiny;
- self-regulation is desirable (to the institutions) but probably not feasible. Effective quality assurance requires the responsible agency to be independent of the institutions it assesses;
- different stakeholders have different purposes and interests in scrutinizing and assessing the quality of institutions and/or provision/outputs. Their requirements, in respect of documentation and access, should not detract from the institution's primary purpose, i.e., to educate students; and

- the tension between the demands of external accountability and quality improvement must be recognized. In the interests of ensuring efficiency and effectiveness, overlap and duplication in the demands of different external agencies should be avoided.

There is no 'correct' model of quality assurance. One approach which might meet the above criteria would be based on the production, on an annual basis, of quality profiles. These would be based around a set of quantitative and qualitative criteria designed to demonstrate institutional effectiveness, specified within the framework of the institutional mission. Performance would be assessed annually against the chosen criteria in a self-assessment by the institution, supported by evidence of student and employer satisfaction. Where appropriate, institutions might choose to draw on some of the quality management tools developed outside of higher education (such as quality function deployment, currently being successfully operated by companies like Toyota) (Finch, 1993) which might tackle the problem of 'the quality burden' by utilizing data for both quality assurance and quality improvement purposes. Reports would be published. In principle, the production of the quality profiles should facilitate inter-institution comparability, at least within clearly defined institutional 'families', i.e., groups of universities with a similar mission, thereby reinforcing the cycle of quality improvement.

What is clear is that quality assurance is in transition. Some countries are only now responding to the demands of accountability by thinking about arrangements for external scrutiny of higher education provision. The more 'mature' countries, dissatisfied with current arrangements, are looking for more effective solutions. There is potential for cooperation and the transfer of good practice. The common cause is the desire to enhance students' experience within higher education and their life chances beyond.

Notes

1 For example, Inspectors formed an important element of the external quality assurance systems to which the UK non-university higher education institutions (Polytechnics and Colleges) were subject prior to the 1992 Further and Higher Education Act. Inspections, which were subject-based, were carried out by an independent agency, Her Majesty's Inspectorate (HMI) which reported to the Secretary of State for Education. While some other countries use the terminology of inspection to describe institutional visits, this rarely involves direct observation of the teaching and learning experience.

2 While quality assessment focuses primarily on the subject or 'cognate area of provision', the approach adopted by the Scottish and English Funding Councils relies on making judgments about the quality of provision within the context of the individual institution's stated mission.

References

ALEXANDER, D. and MORGAN, J. (1992) 'Quality Assurance in a European Context', paper presented to the AETT conference on *Quality in Education*, University of York, 6–8 April.

BALL, C. (1985) *Fitness for Purpose*, Guildford, SRHE and NFER/Nelson.

BLUMER, S.S. and SINCLAIR, R. (1973) 'Chemists in British universities: A study of the reward system in science', in *American Sociological Review*, 38, February, pp. 126–138.

BRENNAN, J., GOEDEGEBUURE, L.C.J., SHAH, T., WESTERHEIJDEN, D.F. and WESTHOF, P.M. (1992) *Towards a Methodology for Comparative Quality Assessment in European Higher Education*, CNAA, CHEPS, HIS, London.

DAVIS, C.G. and STRONZ, R.H. (1985) 'The politics of accreditation and the role of COPA on self-regulation', in BENNETT, J.B. and PELTASON, J.W. (Eds) *Contemporary Issues in Higher Education: Self-regulation and the Ethical Roles of the Academy*, London, Macmillan.

FINCH, J. (1993) 'Quality and its measurement: A business perspective' in GREEN, D. (1993) (Ed) *What is Quality?*, SRHE/OUP.

HARVEY, L., BURROWS, A. and GREEN, D. (1992) *Criteria of Quality*, QHE, Birmingham.

HARVEY, L. and GREEN, D. (1993) 'Defining quality', in *Assessment and Evaluation in Higher Education*, 18, 1, pp. 9–34, Carfax, Bath.

HEALEY, J.S. (1980) 'Accreditation from the other side: A study of the accreditation process and its effects on three schools', in *Journal of Education for Librarianship*, 21, 2.

LLOYD, R. (1992) 'Foreword', in ROBERTS, D. and HIGGINS, T. (1992) Higher Education: The Student Experience: The Findings of a Research Programme into Student Decision Making and Consumer Satisfaction, Leeds, HEIST.

MARCHESE, J. (1991) 'TQM reaches the Academic', in *AAHE Bulletin*, 3–14 November.

MAZELAN, P., BRANNIGAN, C., GREEN, D., TORMEY, P. and O'SHEA, J. (1991) 'Using measures of students satisfaction: The implications of a user-led strategy for quality assurance in Higher Education', in *Broadcast*, 18, Winter, pp. 4–5.

PARASURAMAN, A. *et al.* (1985) 'A conceptual model of service quality and its implications for future research', in *Journal of Marketing*, 49, pp. 41–50.

PIRSIG, R.M. (1976) *Zen and the Art and Motorcycle Maintenance: An Enquiry into Values*, London, Corgi.

REYNOLDS, P.A. (1986) *Academic Standards for Universities*, London, CVCP.

ROBERTS, D. and HIGGINS, T. (Eds) (1992) Higher Education: The Student Experience: The Findings of a Research Programme into Student Decision Making and Consumer Satisfaction, Leeds, HEIST.

SENSICLE, A. (1991) *Quality Assurance in Higher Education: The Hong Kong Initiative*, presented at the HKCAA International Conference on Quality Assurance, Hong Kong, 15–17 July.

WALSH, K. (1991) 'Quality and public services', in *Public Administration*, 69, 4, pp. 503–14.

Chapter 20

Quality Assurance in a Changing World

Jacques L'Ecuyer and Marjorie Peace Lenn

This book presents only a small selection of papers from the 1993 Conference of the International Network of Quality Assurance Agencies in Higher Education (INQAAHE). Here the co-chairs of the Conference review some of the main issues and questions raised in plenary and group sessions during the five-day event.

Quality of Education: A New Interest

That the conference on which this book is based was attended by participants from forty-five countries is an index of current preoccupations with quality in higher education. Many speakers reflected that this is related to the need to consolidate higher education systems after the rapid expansion of the past decades. The creation of new programs and new institutions, and ever-rising costs during this period have raised questions about the value and efficiency of higher education and about ways of assuring its quality. Higher education's major role in developing a nationally competitive economy, and its internationalization are additional factors. Countries want their institutions to produce graduates who will make a competent workforce, well adapted to the challenges of an economy based on knowledge and on technology. There is a demand for people able to use their skills beyond their home country and several professions now have international quality standards.

How do we ensure the quality of systems as the number of students escalates? How can we ensure that the money is invested in the most efficient way possible? How do we ensure that the training programs meet international standards? How do we ensure that the institutions give society the graduates it needs? These matters are at the heart of efforts to develop ways of controlling and assuring the quality of higher education.

The Concept of Quality in Higher Education

The concept of quality does not have the same meaning for everyone, and the Conference drew on two main interpretations. The first requires institutions

178

or programs to meet predetermined standards. Accrediting agencies, particularly those from the professional sector, generally employ such 'objective' measures of quality. The choice of standards or criteria is obviously crucial; they vary in different countries and types of institution but there is increasing reference to international standards, whether achieved formally by agreement between agencies, as in engineering, or indirectly by calling on international experts. Some institutions also seek accreditation by agencies from another country to attest to the international quality of their programs and education.

The second concept of quality relates to institutional mission. An institution is said to be of quality if it achieves its mission and meets the expectations of its stakeholders — the students, the financial backers, and society in general. This involves a judgment both on the pertinence of the mission and on whether it is fulfilled, and it allows for diversity between institutions by letting them choose their mission. It stresses the quality of the 'educative product' as measured by the acquired knowledge of the graduates, their ease in finding work, or their social performance. There is less interest in the process ('teaching') than in the results ('learning'), there are attempts to assess the added value of higher education, and there are links with efforts to implement total quality in university management. The problem is that no one has the same expectations, some being contradictory or difficult to attain at the same time. Nevertheless this approach does put emphasis on results and on students, and is the basis for some very promising initiatives for improving quality in higher education.

Quality in Developing and Newly Industrialized Countries

The difficulties encountered in promoting and ensuring quality in the developing and newly industrialized countries vary from region to region. The phenomenal growth of higher education registrations and the resulting budgetary pressure on this sector's budget has had differing effects. In Africa there is a serious crisis characterized by shortage of material, documentation and, in some cases, the incapacity to pay the academic salaries. Assuring quality in Africa involves the regionalization of educational programs, the creation of institutional networks, and severe limits on the number of places available in the universities. In Asia and Latin America, the private sector has been enlisted to assist with the growth crisis either by charging or raising tuition fees, or by creating private institutions. The World Bank is a strong advocate of this approach; UNESCO points out its limitations. Other measures to meet the demand for higher education include (notably in Asia), the establishment of branch campuses or franchising arrangements by foreign universities, and the development of distance education.

In this context of diversified initiatives, governments must guard the quality of higher education institutions, whether public or private, and put in place the necessary mechanisms to assure society of their value and pertinence.

The Chilean, Mexican and Brazilian experiences in Latin America, Chinese, Taiwanese and Korean in Asia, Romanian and Lithuanian in Eastern Europe, as well as those of Jordan and Egypt were all described during the conference. They illustrated how quality assurance mechanisms must be adapted to each situation and how their development is a long process. This is particularly true when an evaluation 'culture' is not in place or when the traditions of institutional autonomy are very strong.

In Latin America, institutional accreditation similar to that practised in the USA seems to be the model, and some universities even seek accreditation direct from American agencies. Although this model is also found in the Philippines, European inspired models, with stronger government involvement are more often evident in Asia, for example in China, Thailand, Indonesia, and even in Korea and Taiwan. In the Middle East and Eastern Europe governments also play an important role. Malaysia, Singapore, Hong Kong and India have followed the English system which traditionally gave greater freedom to the universities — although, here as elsewhere, governments have been tightening their control during the past decade. In most of these countries, professional or specialized (by program) accreditation is gaining in popularity.

Quality in Industrialized Countries

In the industrialized countries the rising costs of higher education have also brought governments to question the efficiency and quality of institutions. In Europe, North America, Australia and New Zealand there are some common features:

- First of all, the belief that quality must be assured by the institutions themselves, with central agencies ensuring that they meet this responsibility and, where necessary helping them with this. United Kingdom, Australia, New Zealand, the USA, as well as Canada (Quebec) have developed 'audit' systems to verify institutions' own management of quality.
- Where central agencies are used, whether to evaluate institutional management of quality or the educational programs provided, or both, most countries judge it essential for credibility that the organization is independent of government and of the institutions. Confidentiality is still debated although the trend is in favour of a public testimony, in one form or other, of evaluation results.
- The use of procedures which involve an internal self-evaluation by the program or by the institution, followed by a visit by external (increasingly international) experts.
- The growing use of funding to promote or to recognize quality. Australia and some US states, for example, hold back part of funding to encourage their establishments to be attentive to quality matters.

- New emphasis on the verification of the impact of the educational programs on students. Without abandoning the evaluation of resources and the educational process, the effect on students and what they actually learn is rapidly becoming the focal point. In the USA, the existence and use of means to verify student achievement is now often an accreditation criteria or a condition for obtaining certain funds.
- The unification or consolidation of all the quality assurance constituents of a higher education system in one organization. The most striking example, without a doubt, is the New Zealand Qualifications Authority which is responsible for assuring quality in the whole of the post-compulsory education and training sector. In giving one agency the mandate to watch over the quality in varying establishments, very flexible procedures are needed to take into account each one's mission and objectives.

Quality and International Exchanges

Mobility programs in industrialized countries, such as ERASMUS, have extended the development of bilateral relationships between the participating institutions and the generalization of credit transfer systems; mutual recognition and equivalence of standards raise issues that need to be thoroughly studied. As previously noted, in the professional sector there are agreements between the professional corporations and their associated accreditation agencies. Where universities seek recognition from agencies in other countries, there is a risk that the evaluations may not be adapted to the local context and can become a form of cultural imperialism, which may detract from the short-term beneficial effects on the level of education.

Where universities from industrialized countries have established branches or franchised courses in developing countries, the intention is to meet a demand for high-calibre programs which meet international standards. The same concerns about cultural imperialism apply here; and in addition, unless the branches and franchises are in close contact with the lead institutions, the level and quality of programs may not always come up to expectations.

Other Questions

During the conference, external examining and accreditation were closely examined as long-standing quality assurance practices. The former has proved to be very useful for ensuring comparability and equity, and for promoting quality, although the increase in student numbers, the variety of their educational paths and their greater mobility has created some difficulties. Accreditation has long been the cornerstone of the American quality assurance system. However its effectiveness is being called into question, and it seems clear that agencies will have to take a close look at some of their procedures, tighten their standards and better communicate their evaluation results.

Distance education with its very large numbers of part-time students also received attention, and its quality assurance will doubtless gain in importance during the coming years. And although the main focus of the conference (and of this book) was on quality assurance agencies, a number of speakers presented interesting experiences from an institutional perspective.

The diverse origins of the conference participants sensitized them to the influence local contexts have on the nature of the problems and how to tackle them. The differing conditions between rich and poor countries were particularly striking: the former are using ever more sophisticated means to give their higher education system the highest possible level of performance; many of the latter are striving simply to meet a minimum standard of quality for all their institutions. In the context of ever-increasing international exchanges, the formation of the International Network of Quality Assurance Agencies (INQAAHE) with its database, regular Newsletter (QA) and biennial international conferences, and the publication of this selection of papers is intended to support the dissemination of ideas and practices in the assurance and promotion of quality within all forms of higher education.

APPENDIX: Full List of Papers Presented at the Montreal Conference, May 1993

Abecassis, Alain/ Cazenave, Philippe and Hoffert, Michael	La Politique des Contrats État-Universités en France
Arredondo, Victor	Institutional Autonomy and Performance-based Public Financing in Mexico's Higher Education
Ayarza, Hernan	Quality Assurance in Latin American Higher Education: an over-view of university accreditation
Barker, Alan	Quality Assessment and Quality Improvement within Higher Education: the New Zealand perspective
Bauer, Marianne and Franke-Wikberg, Sigbrit	Quality Assurance in Swedish Higher Education: shared responsibility
Beju, Iulian	Développements Récents dans l'Enseignement Supérieur de l'Europe Centrale et de l'Est: mecanismes nationaux de promotion de la qualité
Biron, André	Accreditation of Engineering Programs in Canada and Inter-National Mutual Recognition Agreements
Cauchi, Susan	Quality Measures in the New Environment: familiar issues in a changing world
Cazenave, Philippe	Le programme IMHE de l'OCDE et la Garantie de la Qualité de l'Enseignement Supérieur
Cazenave, Philippe and Staropoli, André	Program on Institutional Management in Higher Education: the development of performance indicators for higher education

Chaloux, Bruce/ Brey, Ronald and Maher, Julianne	Quality Assurance in Distance Learning: strategies and challenges for the 1990s
Cheong, Doreen	System of Quality Assurance of Courses at the Singapore Polytechnic
Craft, Alma	University Mobility in the Asia Pacific Region (UMAP)
Craft, Maurice	External Examining: a review of its rationale and mode of operation
Crow, Steven	Challenges to Accreditation in the United States
Curtis, Sue	Quality Moves in Australian Higher Education
Dias, Marco Antonio	Quality in Higher Education from an International Point of View: the role of UNESCO
Dicks, Dennis and Shaw, Steven	Order from Chaos: applying quality control in academia
Dixon, Thomas	Quality Principles in Academic Staff Selection and Development
Donaldson, James	Quality Assessment in Higher Education Institutions in Scotland
Gagot Huguet, Antonio	Message from Minister of Education, Mexico
Green, Diana	Quality Assurance in Western Europe: trends, practices and issues
Gundacker-Hackl, Elsa and Pechar, Hans	Quality Management in Transition in Austria
Hamel, Claude	Le Systeme Universitaire Québécois et l'Assurance de la Qualité
Harker, Barry	Quality Assurance: an institutional perspective
Harman, Grant	Regional Perspective on Quality Assurance: Asia and the Pacific
Harvey, Lee	Total Student Experience: a first report of the QHE survey
Hébert, Paul	The World Bank and Higher Education: Quality Improvement and Assurance
Hölttä, Seppo	Quality Assurance: a challenge for decentralized management in Finnish higher education
Ifrim, Mircea	Aspects regarding the Accreditation Norms for the Institutions of Higher Education in Romania

Jacobs, Danie	Quality Assurance in Vocational Higher Education in Southern Africa
Jedegwa, Vyson	Quality Assurance in University Education in Southern Africa: the dilemma for Malawi
Jones, Elizabeth	Development of International Faculty Peer Review Model to compare Accounting Programs and Courses
Khanna, S.K. and Sharma, G.D.	Measures of Quality Assurance in Higher Education: an Indian experience
Kohl, Kay and Miller, Gary	Quality Assurance and Transnational Education
L'Abbé, Maurice	La Vérification de l'Évaluation Périodique des Programmes d'Étude dans les Universités du Québec
Lajeunesse, Claude	Academic Mobility and Quality Assurance: the North American context
Lee, Wha-kuk	Issues and Development of University Accreditation in Korea
Lentz, B., Manders, T. and Kalkwijk, J.	Effects of External Quality Assessment on Dutch Universities
Lewis, Richard	The System of External Examining in the United Kingdom: its strengths and weaknesses and the need for change
Li, Jianmin and Wang, Zonglie	Academic Degrees Accreditation and Evaluation in China
Liston, Colleen	The Development of a Theory of Accreditation
Lobo, Pedro	Thoughts about Institutional Evaluation
Lopez, Estela	Reaction of an Institution Submitted to an Accreditation Review
Malcolm, Wilfred	The Development of an Academic Audit Unit in New Zealand
Market, Axel	Quality Assurance and Equivalencies: the international mobility of students, scholars and professionals
Meade, Phil	Recent Development in Quality Assurance in Australian Higher Education: strategies for professional development

Mercado del Collado, Ricardo	The Advancements and Limitations Experienced in the Four Years of Operation of a National Evaluation System for Higher Education: the case of Mexico
Mockiené, Birute	Problems and Concepts on Evaluation of Higher Education and Research Institutions in Lithuania
Morosini, Marília Costa	University Quality by Policy and Assessment of the Faculty
Nadeau, Gilles	L'usage des Indicateurs de Qualité dans les Colleges et les Universités
Nolan, Donald	New York State Review and Approval of Academic Programs within a Tradition of Institutional Autonomy
O'Connor, James	Quality Assurance for Degrees Approved by the New Zealand Qualifications Authority
Owako, Frederick	In Search of Quality in Higher Education in Kenya
Panhelainen, Mauri and Konttinen Raimo	Creating New Strategies: self-evaluation in Finnish higher education
Peace Lenn, Marjorie	International Linkages and Quality Assurance: a shifting paradigm
Ramirez Gatica, Soledad	Quality Control Efforts in Chilean Higher Education: twelve years experience
Ratcliff, James	Student Outcomes Assessment as a means of Quality Assurance
Ribeiro Durham, Eunice	Evaluation Quality and Accountability in Brazilian Higher Education
Roaden, Arliss	Performance Based Funding
Robillard, Lucienne	Address by Minister of Education and Science, Quebec
Salah, Munther	Practices and Issues Related to Quality Assurance in Higher Education in the Arab World
Sensicle, Allan	One country, Two (Education) Systems: a perspective from Hong Kong
Shabani, Juma	L'expérience Africaine dans la Promotion de la Qualité de l'Enseignement Superieur

Short, Keith and Teo, Chiang Liang	Quality Assurance in Inter-National Academic Associations: the franchising of courses from the United Kingdom to Malaysia
Staropoli, André	Le Comité National d'Evaluation: un Organisme Independant pour l'Evaluation des Etablissements d'Enseignement Superieur en France
Strubbé, Jose	Evaluation and Quality-improvement of Education: influences of research activities and results
Strydom, A.H./ Khotseng, B.M.	The Transformation of Universities in South Africa and Approaches to Quality Assurance
Su, Jin-Li	Specialized Accreditation in Taiwan: issues and perspectives
Thomas, Alun	Performance Funding and the English Higher Education Funding Council
Thune, Christian	The Experience with Establishing Procedures for Evaluation and Quality Assurance of Higher Education in Denmark
Torres Mejia, David	Quality Assurance Perspectives on Latin American Higher Education System
Van der Donckt, Pierre	Amélioration et Promotion de la Qualité dans une Perspective Internationale
Van Vught, Frans	Towards a General Model of Quality Assessment in Higher Education
Woodhouse, David	Education as Commerce
Yeates, Maurice	A Decade of Graduate Program Review in Ontario: process and results

(A complete set of papers is available on request from The Conference of Rectors and Principals of the Universities of Quebec (CREPUQ), PO Box 876, Place du Parc Station, Montreal, Quebec, Canada H2W 2P5. The price is $40 Can., including tax and mailing).

Notes on Contributors

Hernan Ayarza is the Associate Director of CINDA (Centro Interuniversitario de Desarrollo), an academic organization of Latin American and Spanish universities. He has been professor of civil engineering and head of the engineering school at the Catholic University of Chile, and the academic vice-rector of the University of Santiago.

Alan Barker taught literature, linguistics and philosophy in universities, and horticulture and apiculture at a polytechnic. He has undertaken social and economic analysis in education for the New Zealand government, and is now in charge of policy, research and development at the New Zealand Qualifications Authority.

Iulian Beju has been a professor of mathematics at the University of Bucharest and is now Director of the Department of Higher Education at the Romanian Ministry of Education. His publications include papers on education systems, assessment and accreditation.

Alma Craft has worked in higher education in England, Australia and Hong Kong. In the UK she was a professional officer with the Schools Council, and the National Curriculum Council. In 1993 she moved from the Hong Kong Council for Academic Accreditation to the University of Greenwich in London.

Steven Crow has been Deputy Director of the Commission on Institutions of Higher Education of the North Central Association of Colleges and Schools in the United States since 1989. Based in Chicago, the Commission is affiliated with over 950 member institutions in nineteen states.

Marco Antonio Dias has been Director of the Division of Higher Education at UNESCO in Paris since 1981, coordinating programmes in higher education, teacher education, research and development. He has worked as a journalist and lawyer in Brazil, has taught philosophy and law, and was vice-rector of the University of Brasilia.

Jim Donaldson became Director of Teaching and Learning in the Scottish Higher Education Council in June 1992, and is a member of the EC group on Quality Assessment in Higher Education. He has taught in further and higher education, and for ten years was a member of Her Majesty's Inspectorate.

Diana Green is Senior Pro-Vice-Chancellor at the University of Central England, and was previously a civil servant, consultant and lecturer. She directs the University's Centre for the Study of Quality in Higher Education, and is a member of the Quality Assessment Committee of the Higher Education Funding Council (England).

Grant Harman is Professor of Educational Administration and Director of the Institute of Public Sector Management at the University of New England, Australia. His main research interests are in higher education policy and management, comparative higher education, and public-sector management and public policy.

Claude Hamel is President of the University of Quebec, and President of the Conference of Rectors and Principals of Quebec Universities. Educated as a civil engineer, he taught at the University of Sherbrooke where he became vice-rector (administration) then rector, before moving to Quebec University.

Paul Hebert was a professor of education in the United States and now acts as a consultant to the Education and Social Policy Department of the World Bank in Washington.

Danie Jacobs is the Executive Director of the Certification Council for Technikon Education (SERTEC) in South Africa. Previously he was a research officer, lecturer and head of department at the Witwatersrand Technikon, then an inspector and planner in the Department of National Education.

Kay Kohl is Executive Director of the National University Continuing Education Association in Washington, DC, an association of colleges and universities founded in 1915 to promote the development of degree- and non-degree higher education opportunities for part-time students.

Jacques L'Ecuyer is now Chairman of the Quebec Commission d'Évaluation de l'Énseignement Collégial. At the time of the conference, he was academic Vice-President of the University of Quebec and President of the Academic Affairs Committee of the Quebec Conference of Rectors and Principals.

Wha-Kuk Lee has a UK doctorate and was professor of chemical education at Chonbuk National University, Korea. He has published widely on science and on higher education, and is currently Director of University Evaluation at the Korean Council for University Education.

Marjorie Peace Lenn is Executive Director of the Center for Quality Assurance in International Education in Washington DC. As well as advising the World Bank, OECD, UNESCO, and OAS she has worked directly with governments in Europe, the Far East, and the United States.

Gary Miller is Assistant Vice-President for Distance Education at the Pennsylvania State University. He was formerly associate vice-president for program development at the University of Maryland University College, and executive director of the International University Consortium.

Soledad Ramirez-Gatica is an associate professor and a former dean and vice-president for academic affairs at the Universidad del Bio-Bio, Concepcion, Chile. Her research area is quality control in institutions of higher education, and she is a consultant to the Chilean Council of Education.

Juma Shabani was born and educated in Burundi. He has a Russian master's degree in mathematics and a doctorate in physics from Belgium. He was deputy vice-chancellor at the University of Burundi before being appointed in 1992 as Deputy Secretary of the Association of African Universities.

Keith Short has worked in universities in the USA, the UK and Ireland, and in 1983 was appointed as professor of life sciences at Nottingham Polytechnic, UK (now the Nottingham Trent University). He is now Deputy Vice-Chancellor with particular responsibility for academic planning and quality assurance.

Teo Chiang Liang is Executive Director and a governor of Kolej Bandar Utama, a private college in Malaysia offering tertiary education. The college has links with US universities and a twinning arrangement with Nottingham Trent University.

Christian Thune is Director of the Centre for Quality Assurance and Evaluation of Higher Education. Previously he was professor of international politics at the University of Copenhagen. He chaired the Committee of Chairmen of the Danish Education Councils, and also the committee which reviewed the Danish system of external examiners.

Frans van Vught is a professor of public administration and Director of the Centre for Higher Education Policy Studies (CHEPS) at the University of Twente in the Netherlands. He has published extensively on higher education, and has been a consultant for the EC, OECD, UNESCO and the World Bank.

Index